Endo

Do you want to only arrive at a destination, or do you enjoy the sights along the way? For some, the goal is the final destination; for others, the goal is the journey along the way. Do you want to read a unique book about "seeing in the Holy Spirit?" Using a storyboard style delivery, Ana Werner depicts a journey of a seer from point A to point Z with many amazing stops along the way. You will learn the A, B C's of the Starting Gate, and you will also be given a prophetic glimpse of the finished word of the Cross of Jesus in this captivating read.

DR. JAMES W. GOLL
Bestselling author of *The Seer, Dream Language,*
and *Lifestyle of a Prophet*
Founder of God Encounters
International Author and Minister
Life Language Communications Trainer

I like the way Ana writes. She is a visionary, and yet has a practical writing style that makes the invisible, spiritual world something a sincere believer can experience. I recommend *The Seer's Path* and look forward to future books as the Lord further instructs her.

Hal Linhardt
Director
Kansas City Evangelists' Fellowship

I highly recommend this book. It will challenge you and put a desire in your heart to draw closer to God. I picked it up to read a few chapters, and it so captivated me that I read the whole book! I loved it!"

CAROL KOCH
Children on the Frontlines Director

It is my pleasure to recommend to you Ana Werner's book *The Seer's Path*. Reading through the pages, I had one word that kept coming to me as descriptive of the heart of this book and the major impact that it will have on you, the reader. That word is "practical." Seeing is practical, and this book gives practical insights into how you can see! You will come to grips with just how important the whole area of seeing into the spiritual realm is. Seeing what God is doing is biblical, it is real. Seeing is how our Bible heroes functioned, and how they could do all that they did. Jesus has purposed, destined, and equipped us to see in this arena. Ana gives insights into how this has influenced her daily life. Then she provides applications and help for us to flow in this area as well. Finally, each chapter concludes with powerful prayers of release that as you agree with them, will literally happen! You will experience a release, an unlocking to be a seer!

There is another reason that I can recommend this book so highly. I know the Werners. They are a vital part of the church I pastor and I know their character. I not only recommend the content of the book, I recommend the author! The Seer's path is a great read and even better application.

ALAN KOCH
Founding pastor of Christ Triumphant Church

It is with certainty of character and giftings that I recommend Ana Werner to you! Seeing in the Spirit comes with revelation and responsibility, Ana knows and understands "to whom much is given, much is required" (Luke 12:48). Her book does a remarkable job of helping others understand and grow in revelatory ways. Thank you Ana!

LAURIE DITTO
Evangelist, Seer, Author,
Producer, Director & Founder of My Father's Reputation

The Holy Spirit gives gifts as He desires, and Ana Werner is gifted as a seer. You will enjoy Ana's experiences with the angelic and the Lord; she will convince you that there is more to this Christian life then you are experiencing now. Maybe you didn't meet your guardian angel when you were five years old; she did. Maybe you have never been interrupted while doing dishes and have an angel knock on your door and make an appointment with you for later when your little daughter was taking her nap; she has. We know and love Ana, her husband, and her children. She is as real as your next door neighbor, but she experiences the supernatural in a way that will challenge and change your life. We heartily recommend this enriching book that will help you on your own supernatural journey with the Lord.

DORIS AND LEE HARMS
Heartland Healing Rooms

the
seer's
path

the
seer's
path

AN INVITATION TO EXPERIENCE HEAVEN, ANGELS, AND THE INVISIBLE REALM OF THE SPIRIT

ANA WERNER

DESTINY IMAGE® PUBLISHERS, INC.
P.O. Box 310, Shippensburg, PA 17257-0310
"Promoting Inspired Lives."

This book and all other Destiny Image and Destiny Image Fiction books are available at Christian bookstores and distributors worldwide.

Cover design by Eileen Rockwell
Interior design by Terry Clifton

For more information on foreign distributors, call 717-532-3040.
Reach us on the Internet: www.destinyimage.com.

ISBN 13 TP: 978-0-7684-1070-9
ISBN Hardcover: 978-0-7684-1461-5
ISBN Large Print: 978-0-7684-1460-8
ISBN 13 eBook: 978-0-7684-1071-6

For Worldwide Distribution, Printed in the U.S.A.
1 2 3 4 5 6 7 8 / 21 20 19 18 17

Dedication

This book is dedicated to my loving husband—for always believing in me and cheering me on. To my parents, family and friends: thank you for all your support, prayers, and encouragement.

Contents

Chapter 1

What's a Seer?

"What's a seer?" my husband asked me on one of our very first dates.

"Well, I'm a seer. It's like a person who sees in the spiritual realm with Jesus. Kind of like a prophet. I see angels; in fact, one has been with us from the beginning of our relationship and is sitting in the back seat right now."

"Like, *now*?" my husband responded in shock.

"Yes, now."

"Well, what's he saying?" my husband asked with curiosity.

Five years ago, the Lord took me on a journey of giving me a language for explaining what seer anointing truly is. Back then, when I first met my husband, I didn't really have the clear understanding or the courage to explain or teach on it that I do now. For years, I just had all these incredible encounters and experiences with the Lord in ministry and in heaven, but never did I have clear biblical understanding of what this gift from God truly was.

My husband's question that day actually launched me into discovering what this "seer anointing" really was and how I could explain it and teach on it in a simplified way for people to understand.

What Does the Bible Say?

Examining the Scriptures, I found that a *seer* is actually in the Bible. In fact, it's actually many times in the Bible. Look it up yourself! In this day and age, we have the amazing ability to type a word into the computer and do a search. Always cross reference what you will find online, though, with the actual Word of God.

In 1 Samuel 9, Saul's father is in distress because his donkeys have gone missing. Saul and one of his servants go searching everywhere for them. After a long time of looking without success, they decide to try one last thing. *"Behold now, there is a man of God in this city, and the man is held in honor; all that he says surely comes true. Now let us go there, perhaps he can tell us about our journey on which we have set out"* (1 Sam. 9:6 NASB). *"Come, and let us go to the seer"* (1 Sam. 9:9 NASB).

So they go to meet Samuel with the intention to receive some wisdom about how to find these donkeys, but God actually has set up a divine appointment for Saul in this meeting.

The seer Samuel sees Saul in the distance and God tells him, *"Behold, the man of whom I spoke to you! This one shall rule over My people"* (1 Sam. 9:17 NASB).

Saul approaches Samuel, and before he can even explain the donkeys Samuel invites him to come and get refreshed, eat some food with him, and get some rest. Then Samuel the seer says, "Oh and by the way, those donkeys that you are looking for—don't worry about them, they've been found." Imagine Saul's shock at the prophetic anointing on this guy! Later on, Samuel anoints Saul as King of Israel.

God uses seers like Samuel to speak prophetically into people's lives. Seers *see* and then prophesy. People sought out seers in the Bible for wisdom and counsel. Often, though, seers came uninvited to prophesy into a powerful person's life. God uses a bold seer named Gad to speak strong words to King David that radically change Israel (see 2 Sam. 24). Seers were used in the Bible to radically bring about shift and change.

Seers hear from the Lord primarily through the gift of seeing and then declare things to come.

> *He then stationed the Levites in the house of the Lord with cymbals, with harps and with lyres, according to the command of David and of Gad the king's seer, and of Nathan the prophet; for the command was from the Lord through his prophets* (2 Chronicles 29:25 NASB).

Here, there is a distinction between seers and prophets. As confusing as this sounds, all seers can prophesy, but not all prophets can see. Out of the five fold ministry that is mentioned in the Bible, a seer falls under the office of a prophet (see Eph. 4). It's a prophet with the ability or gift of seeing in the spiritual realm.

And He gave some as apostles, and some as prophets, and some as evangelists, and some as pastors and teachers, for the equipping of the saints for the work of service, to the building up of the body of Christ (Ephesians 4:11-12 NASB).

The Start

The scripture that was prophesied over my life was, "He had a dream, and behold, a ladder was set on the earth with its top reaching to heaven; and behold, the angels of God were ascending and descending on it" (Gen. 28:12 NASB). Jacob falls into a deep sleep at a place that he later names Bethel. In his dream, heaven is opened to him and he has the ability to see angels ascending and descending upon the earth, and he sees the Lord. So this was the word prophesied over me—essentially, that I would be able to see the supernatural things of God.

At five years old, I saw my first angel. He just showed up one day in my room while I was playing. From what I remember, I didn't feel threatened or scared by this random angel in my room but felt incredible peace with him. He was dressed in white, had a warm glow about him, and had four wings. I remember asking him if I could touch his wings, and he let me. After we played together for a bit, he told me before he left that he was my guardian angel and that God sent him to always protect me.

After that one encounter, I never saw into the supernatural again until I was 22 and living in Brazil as a missionary. I don't know why; for years seeing was locked for me. However, once it did open for me to see the things of God again, I trained in it.

> God doesn't just give us a gift like seeing, prophesying, or evangelizing and then not call us to train in it. Like any profession, we have to keep training in the things of God. It's training to reign with Him!

In 1 Corinthians 12, Paul exhorts the body of Christ to pursue all the gifts: *"earnestly desire the greater gifts"* (1 Cor. 12:31 NASB). Maybe you're thinking, *Wow this all sounds great, but the gift of seeing in the spirit is just not for me!* I encourage you, you're wrong! We are all called to pursue all the gifts, and this includes seeing.

God doesn't just give us a gift like seeing, prophesying, or evangelizing and then not call us to train in it. Like any profession, we have to keep training in the things of God. It's training to reign with Him! Doctors are constantly having to refocus, brush up on their skills, better their abilities, and learn new techniques. It's how they stay challenged, fresh at their skill, and capable to assist others. In just the same way, we need to train in the gift God has given each of us.

Tips to Seeing in the Spirit

Get into His Presence

Often I get asked if it's important to be focusing on the Lord, or in a worship mode, to be able to see in the Spirit. My answer is always the same—no and yes. While it helps to hear and see with the Lord if you are in a quiet, contemplative state, sometimes He likes to surprise me, and I'll randomly be allowed to see something in the spiritual realm when I am not thinking about God at all.

Just the other day, I was doing dishes from the morning's breakfast and was thinking about how I wished I could have more personal time and hoped my daughter would take her nap without a fight that day. I heard a random knock at the door. I opened the door, and there before me was an angel standing in a top hat carrying a briefcase. He told me that he wanted to meet with me that day but that he would come back once my daughter went down for her nap! And he did!

So yes, God shows seers things sometimes when we are not even expecting it, but more often than not it helps to be focusing on the Lord and getting into His presence to see into the supernatural.

Keep Your Eyes Pure

Keeping our eyes pure is so important to walking in the supernatural. Especially as a seer, we have to keep a careful watch on what we allow ourselves to see. The enemy can really strike down our gifting by unwholesome things entering our eye gates. I have to be very careful what I watch in movies or on television, so I make sure that I keep my eyes pure. If you think of your eyes like literal gates, what you allow them to see or open up to is also what you are allowing into your temple. Violence, sexual perversion, jealousy, and lust have no place in the temple of God, and our bodies are His temple.

Often we are victims of the sinful world around us. Accidents happen, and we just end up seeing something that we did not intend to. When our team from the International House of Prayer went down to Mardi Gras to do ministry, often the guys came back feeling victimized by sights they did not want to open themselves up to. We would all gather together and pray for the Lord to cleanse our minds, thoughts, emotions, and eyes after ministry times. As we go out and minister, we are covered by the blood of the Lamb and do not walk in fear. It is always good, though, to be aware of areas the enemy might try to assault us with, and our eyes are the number-one place the enemy will try.

However, it is ridiculous to believe that someone cannot see in the supernatural because their eyes have fallen into sin. While I do think that it is very difficult to be flowing in the gifts of the Spirit while walking in sin, I would never argue that this is an explanation for why someone cannot see. The flowing of the gifts does come easier to those who are trying to live their lives more in touch with Father and more like His very nature. As believers, we need to keep our eyes pure and focused on Him.

Lord, I want to repent for any time I have allowed my eyes to see something that is impure. Anything that I watched, willingly or unwillingly, that was not of You, I want to repent for it right now. I want to repent for any time my eyes have desired something before they desired You. Please forgive me for any time I had an idol in my life that I pursued with my time and energy before I pursued You. Cleanse my eyes, God, so that they may be pure and pleasing to You. Amen.

Get Intimate

Currently, how to do you relate to God? Do you see Him as the Father? Do you see Him as Jesus? Do you see Him as Holy Spirit? Often, the seer realm will be opened to you by one person of the Trinity coming to invade your life. In Brazil when my eyes were first opened, at the time I was relating mostly to God as Jesus. I was needing a friendship with God more than anything, and Jesus came to me often as my friend. I would start having visions in broad daylight of Jesus and me hanging out at a shoreline. From those split-second impressions or visions, my eyes opened up further as God continued to encounter me there. Slowly, Jesus would not only take me into a vision, but I would also be able to interact with Him and then smell the seashore.

Often, people are seeking crazy encounters or life-changing visions (which are incredibly awesome), but seeing in the spiritual realm doesn't always happen like that for everyone. Sometimes it just starts with seeing Father God come and hug you, and that's it—the same vision over and over. From that, as you progress further in seeing in the Spirit, God will take you to more places and open your eyesight into the supernatural. God is not after having a supernatural mind-blowing experience with you; He's after intimacy!

Keep Asking

Ask to see more each time! In the Bible, Daniel was a seer. In Daniel 7, God takes Daniel up into the most incredible vision of his lifetime, ever! The Lord shows Daniel what will happen in the end times, and he also sees the archangel Gabriel!

Seers are always curious people by nature. In Daniel 7, it says "*I kept looking*" repeatedly. So it's not like God just gives Daniel the full vision and explanation at once! God gives him little bits and pieces with explanation, and then God meets Daniel's curiosity and shows him a little more and a little more as Daniel steps out in faith.

Every time I have seen new things in heaven or in the spiritual realm, I always ask to see more! I also ask if I can come back again! When I've been in rooms of heaven, I not only try and see what's there to see, but I try to use all my senses to experience what God has for me. I smell if there is any fragrance in the room; I hear what noises are in the room; I touch whatever I can and also pay attention to my inward senses— what emotion I am feeling in the room.

Glimpses

Finally, don't look down on small beginnings. Not everyone starts seeing a full battlefield in the spiritual realm right away! (Occasionally, there are a few rare people who do.) After my second angelic encounter in Brazil, I didn't see angels with real clarity again for quite some time. I would see just brief instances of them. During worship at church, I would just see a quick image of a wing brushing by, or I would see a glowing blue light standing behind someone. Sometimes I would just see a small flash of light fluttering through the air. I continued to look though! Every time I sensed the Lord's presence falling in a place, I would first pray and ask the Lord to open my eyes, and then I would look around the room and see if I could catch a small glimpse of His presence. The more and more I looked for Him and the more I came with expectation in my heart to see something, the more the Lord would reveal to me. This is how we train our spiritual eyes to see. Come with expectation and curiosity.

Write It Down

Write it down! Everything, *everything* you see, write down. Sometimes God would show me something, and I would have no idea or revelation of what that was about. I'd write it down though. Two months later or sometimes even a year later, I would be at a conference or a meeting, and the main speaker would share about a crazy experience they had with the Lord, and lo and behold it was my same experience. They would then explain the revelation God gave them about that, and then I would have understanding. So write it all down!

Don't feel discouraged if, when you start seeing, you don't understand the vision or encounter. Also, don't be quick to label your experience as not of God because you don't understand it. God often gives revelation to me later after an encounter.

Activation Prayer

God, we are in love with You. Jesus, I just pray that You would show me more of who You are. I want to know You, God. Would You show me Your nature? Please, Lord, open my spiritual eyes to see You more. God, I long to see what it is You see! I long to feel what You feel! Lord, help all my senses come alive to You. There is no one like You, God. How magnificent You are! Holy Spirit, I pray that You would come into this time right now and rest upon me. Thank You, God, that You will only show me what I am supposed to see. Thank You, Lord. Amen.

(Now, wait on the Lord to show you something. Don't forget to ask the Lord to take you or show you this again, and a little bit more next time!)

Discussion Question

1. Do you relate to God as a Father, Jesus a friend, or as Holy Spirit? Ask Him to open your eyes and encounter you this week as one of these and write it down!

Jesus: friend

Holy Spirit: comforter, gifts, fruits, helper,

Chapter 2

Chasing Angels

Often I get asked when I first started really seeing more into the spirit. Besides seeing my first angel at the age of five, I don't really remember seeing more after that until I lived in Brazil. At the age of 22 and fresh out of college, I felt the Lord calling me to move to the country of Brazil with Youth With a Mission and work with street children in the drug trafficking slums of Belo Horizonte. I remember how most colleagues of mine I graduated with voiced how they thought I was absolutely crazy. Most of them (actually, maybe all of them) had plans post-college to reenter the world of school to further their degrees in PhD programs or go for a Masters. I remember at my cum laude dinner for the graduates making a speech about how it was better to follow God's plans for my life than follow the ways of the world. (Pretty bold for a 22-year-old!)

So, fearlessly I went! Well, not exactly fearlessly, but I liked to tell myself that I was! Little did I know how flipped upside down my world would become. I found myself in a vivacious culture, unable to understand any of the language and people around me, working with tough street children who had probably seen more violence than I had ever seen in my life. Here I thought that I was going to change the world! In reality, Brazil changed me! The kids I worked with forever transformed my life. As I learned the language, I was able to work with the children—counseling them, and speaking truth and love into their lives. I learned the hard reality of what love truly looks like sometimes. My life was transformed by the two years I spent there. To this day, I have such a heart for street children.

It was in this place of being a single, young, Caucasian woman working and living in the drug trafficking slums that Jesus opened my eyes in a deeper way! Just to paint a picture of what it was like living there, I will share a story. One day I was waiting at the top of a hill to catch a bus that would take me to the church I attended. Naïvely, I thought that because I had lived in the country for a year already, spoke the language, and knew the slum, there would be no need to worry about waiting alone for a bus. A lady came and sat down next to me and began to chat. I talked with her for a while, but she was pretty intoxicated and reeked of alcohol, so I didn't chat long. The lady crossed the street and sat down near a group and started talking to them. That side of the street marked the beginning of a more dangerous slum known in the area. I knew that but still didn't feel any fear. (I know the Lord has protected me with angels so many times as I've walked away from many dangerous situations unharmed!)

Anyway, as I sat curiously watching this lady flaunt her body about and talk loudly to a group of men, suddenly something shocking happened. Another group of men came from around the corner, one carrying a huge ice block. The group held her against the cement and beat her head in with the ice block! I'd never seen anything like it! As I ran all the way back to my house, I just kept telling myself, *That doesn't just happen! Things like this don't just happen! That lady was just murdered right in front of my eyes! I just talked to her!* Obviously, I had heard stories and knew that murder and violence are so common in the slums, but seeing it made it a reality. This was the environment I lived in as a single missionary.

It was when I first arrived, though, that my spiritual eyes were opened more. (I won't share any more violent stories! I promise.) I had been there only two weeks. I hardly spoke the language. In my broken Portuguese I could say, "Hello, my name is Ana. How are you?" One day, I spent that night at a friend's house. A couple of us girls had a get-together. Everyone else was sleeping in the next morning, but I really couldn't sleep, so I naïvely (again) thought, *I'll just walk home.*

About five blocks into walking home, I was completely lost! Not only was I lost, but I didn't know where I was going. I didn't have the street address of where I lived, a phone number to contact, or even a phone to use. So I kept walking and walking and walking. Eventually, I ended up in a neighborhood that didn't look too friendly. Boys who looked only eight or nine years old were carrying huge guns and staring at me with hatred in their eyes. Even though they were just kids, I was terrified of them.

So I started praying! Boy did I pray! I kept walking, desperately hoping that something familiar would catch my eye, but it didn't. I turned a corner and got to a street where men carrying guns now were making drug deals. I prayed, "God make me invisible! God make me invisible!" Well, He didn't! The men turned and looked at me curiously, like, *What doesn't belong in this picture?* One started to approach me, and at that point I just ran! I ran and ran until I got six blocks away where I found a street with no people.

At this point, I just sat down and cried! Yep, I admit it! There I was, this brave (or so I thought) 22-year-old college graduate, in all my glory, sitting on a cement street corner crying. "Oh, Lord," I cried, "You've got to save me! I'm so lost. I'm so stupid, and I'm so lost! Please help me get home! I don't even know where home is, but please, Lord, help me! Where are You?"

Then, once I stopped my sobbing, I heard Him. It was nothing profound, just one simple phrase. "Look up!" I heard the Lord say.

So I did. To my surprise, I saw an angel at the end of block smiling at me. People always ask me, *What did it look like?* The angel I saw that day was probably seven feet tall, was dressed in a glowing robe, and had huge wings that went high about his head and touched the floor. I never could see his face distinctly, but just could make out his smile. The angel looked at me, laughed, and did the oddest thing. He dropped the flower he was carrying in his hand at the end of the block and ran off.

In that moment, all I knew to do was to chase the angel. *Anywhere he's going has got to better than here!* I thought. I ran to the spot where the flower was and picked it up. I turned the corner and saw my angel ahead of me quite far at the next corner. He dropped another flower. "Follow him," was all I heard the Lord say in that moment. So I did! This kept going on and on for what seemed like an hour. I would run, catch up to him enough to pick up a flower, and then he would disappear around the next corner and I would chase after him. Eventually, the last flower dropped was on my doorstep! An hour later, I was safely at home. Imagine everyone's surprise when they asked me how I managed to find my way home and I responded, "I followed an angel." I still have those flowers pressed in my journal from Brazil today.

Why Study Biblical Angels

I find it appalling that the modern-day church doesn't discuss angels more often. The Bible gives us a record of encounters when angels showed up before Jesus' birth, during His years on this earth, and after His ascension. If the Bible is the holy written Word of God and if angels are in it, then they must be a point of interest God wants us to study. Of course, the study of angels should never precede our study of Jesus. Just as there are recoded in the Bible an archangel and a messenger angel, I believe angels hold different jobs and offices. Here are some of the different types of angels I have encountered.

Warning Angels

Warning angels are simply that! They are angels sent by God to warn His people. In Genesis 19, two angels show up to warn Lot of the terrible destruction that is about to fall on Sodom and Gomorrah. *"Get them out of here, because we are going to destroy this place. The outcry to the Lord against its people is so great that he has sent us to destroy it"* (Gen. 19:12-13 NIV).

Now, why would the Lord care to warn Lot? If He was planning on wiping out an entire city anyway, why would He send angels to warn a specific family to leave before the devastation hit? In His mercy, because of His relationship with Abraham (Lot's brother), he saved Lot and his family (see Gen. 19:29).

Another well-known angel that comes with warning is Joseph's angel. The King Herod had been on a rampage to find and destroy Jesus, the child who was prophesied about who would rule the people of Israel. An angel comes to Joseph in a dream. *"'Get up,' he said, 'take the child and his mother and escape to Egypt. Stay there until I tell you, for Herod is going to search for the child to kill him'"* (Matt. 2:13 NIV). So once again we see God intercepting and sending a warning angel to change the course of history.

I myself have never encountered a warning angel. I like to think, though, that the first angel I saw in Brazil protected me and kept me from danger.

Messenger Angels

God also sent angels that carried a message in the Bible. Gabriel the archangel comes to Mary at a pivotal time in her life.

> *Do not be afraid, Mary; you have found favor with God. You will conceive and give birth to a son, and you are to call him Jesus. He will be great and will be called the Son of the Most High. The Lord God will give him the throne of his father David, and he will reign over Jacob's*

descendants forever; his kingdom will never end (Luke 1:30-33 NIV).

Wasn't that wonderful of God to send an angel to Mary at what could have been the scariest time in her whole life! Gabriel came and delivered a message of hope and encouragement to Mary. The Lord so lovingly knew she would need hope and encouragement to face carrying the Son of God in her womb, not to mention having to go back and explain her pregnancy to her family and Joseph.

Warring Angels

The Bible also describes angels that fight or war on our behalf. In a despairing time and at the end of a twenty-one day fast, Daniel has a crazy vision and encounters a brilliant angel. In Daniel 10, the angel tells him:

> *Do not be afraid, Daniel. Since the first day that you set your mind to gain understanding and to humble yourself before your God, your words were heard, and I have come in response to them. But the prince of the Persian kingdom resisted me twenty-one days. Then Michael, one of the chief princes, came to help me, because I was detained there with the king of Persia* (Daniel 10:12-13 NIV).

This scripture brings so much comfort. Its contents show us that God hears our prayers even if we can't see His answer to them yet. God hears our prayers! Isn't that awesome?

Michael is described as an angel that came and helped Daniel's angels fight off a demonic power. This was no little demon either! It was so strong that it kept Daniel's angel detained for a twenty-one day battle. The archangel Michael must have been one giant angel! Thankfully, the Lord sends us angels to battle for us when we are weak!

Explanation Angels

Then there are those angels that show up in the Bible just to give revelation to people. You can imagine the disciples of Christ scratching their heads, thinking, "Huh? What just happened?" as Jesus leaves in a cloud up to heaven. Jesus ascends and the disciples are standing there "*looking intently up into the sky as he was going*" (Acts 1:10 NIV). They are still staring up into the sky when two angels show up behind them to explain it all. Isn't it refreshing that even the disciples, who spent all their time with Jesus, often just didn't get it! It brings us hope as we sometimes miss all that God has for us in the Scriptures.

> *"Men of Galilee," they said, "why do you stand here looking into the sky? This same Jesus, who has been taken from you into heaven, will come back in the same way you have seen him go into heaven"* (Acts 1:11 NIV).

"Ahhh!" they responded. (No, I just added that in.) It's like revelation sunk in! The Lord was so gracious to send them angels to explain everything. I wonder if He was sitting in heaven watching them staring at the clouds, and He looked at His angels and said, "Geez! Would you guys go down there and explain it to them?"

Personal Testimony of Encountering an Explanation Angel

When my husband and I were dating, as you can imagine I had a fun time describing the seer anointing to him. Now although my husband walks in a strong gifting of discernment and teaching, he doesn't see in the spiritual realm. So just imagine what it was like on our first dates together, as we'd be driving in the car, and I would tell him that an angel just showed up in the backseat! (I think at first he thought I was a little crazy, although he'll never admit that now.)

Right before we got engaged, I kept having these weird encounters with God. I kept seeing old-fashioned looking keys everywhere. During worship, I saw them fall into my hands; I saw them on buildings; I had a real one show up in my drawer and even in my Bible one day! God was definitely trying to teach me something during this time about unlocking my heart.

The day he proposed, Sam took me to my favorite beach in the whole world. I'll never forget the scene of the ocean and beach that day. It was beautiful! The sunset was magnificent; the waves were perfect. We sat praying together and squishing the sand between our toes. Then, I looked up into the sky and saw keys falling. Hundreds and hundreds of keys! "Sam, there's keys falling everywhere," I yelled in glee at him.

"That's awesome!" he responded. "I'm gonna set the camera up to take a picture of our silhouettes in the sunset with the ocean in front of us, OK?" he said. "So stay right there so I can focus the camera."

So I sat just enamored, looking at the hundreds of keys falling while he was behind me fidgeting with the camera. *What in the world, God!* I thought. Then suddenly, a huge angel, at least 20 feet tall, approached me carrying an enormous key in his hand! He offered it to me.

"Sam, there's a huge angel in front of me. He just gave me the biggest key I've ever seen!" I said.

"That's great, Ana! Can you turn around and look at me now?" he said. I turned around and there he was holding a ring proposing to marry me! Flash! Just then the camera behind us took the picture and captured our special moment.

> **Unless it provokes us to desire to see the same gifts, signs, and wonders manifesting in our lives, it's just an inspirational story without carrying any impartation.**

To this day, I think that angel was a gift from the Lord. The Lord was definitely trying to explain to me that my heart was about to be fully opened to my future husband. The Lord and my husband alone carry that key to my heart. It was so precious of the Lord to send an angel to explain it to me that day!

I Want to See Angels Too!

Often my friends ask me, "How do I see angels? I want to see angels too, but I'm not a seer!" First Corinthians 14:1 says, *"Follow the way of love and eagerly desire gifts of the Spirit, especially prophecy*" (NIV). It says that we are to desire the gifts—plural. This means that all the gifts of the Holy Spirit are available to us and we are supposed to eagerly go after them! Although it's encouraging to hear stories and testimonies of God doing amazing signs and wonders through others' lives, unless it provokes us to desire to see the same gifts, signs, and wonders manifesting in our lives it's just an inspirational story without carrying any impartation.

So I always encourage people to go after seeing angels! Sometimes angels don't just show up like, "*Boom!* Here I am!" There have been times when I've just seen glimpses of angels dancing or moving through the room during a church service or during worship. I may just see flashes of light moving about the room. Other times, I've seen glimpses of their wing tips fluttering, and then it's gone. Also, sometimes I have seen an appearance of a glowing shadow behind speakers, and I know that is an angelic presence.

Angelic encounters can also be in closed visions and dreams. Many times, with my eyes shut during worship I'll see an image of an angel moving toward me or planted somewhere in the room on guard. Or, with my eyes closed, I'll have a vision of an angelic presence walking by me or coming up behind me.

What Do I Do Now?

If by reading this you are realizing that perhaps you are starting to see angels, what do you do now? It's been my experience that God doesn't just open our spiritual eyes to see into the supernatural unless there is a purpose.

Often when I've seen warring angels who are dressed in full armor, it causes me to start praying stronger because I know the enemy is on the move. I also always try to ask angels their names. There is significance in names—we can see that biblically! In some encounters, the angel will share with me its name, and it usually has significance to what God is trying to teach me through the encounter; other times the angel doesn't.

Angelic presence should always cause us to worship and glorify God more. Let's not get so fascinated with the supernatural that we miss the purpose of it!

I also have some pretty crazy testimonies of interesting experiences I've had with angels. Once I was praying over this lady during a prophetic conference, and an angel showed up behind her carrying a large trumpet in one hand. A crazy idea came to my mind—I grabbed her right hand, and with my other hand I reached out and touched the wing of the angel. Instantly, the power of God fell on her in a mighty way and she was thrown across the room five feet onto the floor. The angel then winked at me, walked over to where she lay, and blew the trumpet over her. As it blew the trumpet, the lady shared with me later, she was instantly taken up into a vision of heaven through a wind tunnel with the Lord. The angel was clearly sent to release and usher her into the presence of God in a powerful way.

It was during my time as a missionary in Brazil that my eyes were opened to see a whole battlefield of war occurring. I would see angels and demons warring over a whole *favela* (slum) and could see the demonic strongholds that were holding authority in certain areas on the mountaintop.

Whenever God opened my eyes to see these war fields, I was provoked to pray and ask God to release more warring angels. First Corinthians 6:3 says *"Do you not know that we will judge angels?"* (NIV). We have the ability in Jesus' name to ask for the release of ministering angels into any situation!

Angelic presence should always cause us to worship and glorify God more. Let's not get so fascinated with the supernatural that we miss the purpose of it! Worship and praise should be the result every time we experience an angelic encounter. Revelation 4 describes how in heaven there are actual seraphim that surround the throne and just worship the Lord day and night. How much more should we be led to worship Him, who is the only one worthy, after having an angelic encounter!

Activation

There are certain steps to having an angelic encounter that I recommend.

1. Try personalizing and praying the following activation prayer daily, and also ask a mentor to be praying for you to have angelic encounters.

2. If you can find someone who has been known to see angels, ask them to pray over you and impart to you this gift. It says in the Bible to go after the gifts, right? Well then, get courageous and boldly go and ask that person to pray for you. (I recommend this for desiring any of the different gifts.)

3. Angelic activity is often present during powerful worship. I can't tell you how many times I have seen angels dancing around when worship is present! Worship ushers us into the presence of the King, so either start worshiping and praising or play some strong worship music.

4. Begin to get curious! Close your eyes. Once you've been able to get into a meditative state, ask the Lord to show you a vision of an angel. If you have a hard time getting away from your own thoughts and are feeling distracted, turn off the lights in the room. Note down if you sense any presence. Often people have shared with me that they could sense angelic presence before they could see it. This might be your starting point also. Now, try opening your eyes, wherever you are, and see if you can see or sense anything in the room. Even if it's a small start, note it down. Great things come from small beginnings! Next time you try to encounter an angel, see if you can see the same thing and ask the Lord to reveal to you a little more. Note down anything you sense or encounter, including visions or dreams you may have. Ask God also for angelic encounters in your dreams too!

5. If you have an angelic encounter, ask the angel his/her name. Often the names have meaning and might give insight. My angel that was with my husband and me during our dating relationship was named Timothy, which meant *honoring God*.

Activation Prayer

Precious Lord, right now I just ask You to fill the reader with wonderment, curiosity, and childlike faith to begin to see and encounter angels. As You have opened my eyes time and time again to see into the supernatural and witness angels, I pray that there would be an impartation that happens right now in the spirit of the person reading this book. I pray for a release of angelic activity around the reader.

Lord, increase their dream life also. I pray for supernatural surprises for the reader. Lord, release Your angels to come and encounter this person.

Even now I pray against and bind any form of warfare that may be presently blocking their senses from experiencing the supernatural in the blood of the Lamb. Father, increase their sensitivity to Your presence. Open their spiritual eyes to see more right now in the name of Jesus Christ. We love You and thank You, God. Amen.

Chapter 3

Spiritual Armor: The Garment of Praise

I want to preface this chapter by admitting my own insecurity to share my thoughts on spiritual armor. If you were to walk into a Christian bookstore, you could find a whole section devoted to this subject, as there have already been so many marvelous books written on this topic. In all honesty though, no matter how many times I read on the topic of spiritual armor, it wasn't until I found myself in situations where I really needed to live out the concepts, that I learned anything. So I am writing from what I've personally been challenged with and had to pursue and add to my lifestyle. Hopefully my own story won't be just another piece of writing on the subject matter for you.

In 2011, my husband and I went to Mozambique, Africa to be missionaries and learn under Heidi and Rolland Baker. We had been married just one year and were already both experienced missionaries, but little did we know just how challenged we would be. Pemba, Mozambique was unlike any other place I had ever been to. Besides the lack of living space and constant dirt and bugs, the heat of Africa in October seemed to drain our ability to do much but just lay in the presence of the Almighty—which was wonderful! I would recommend anyone go and work with the Bakers if you get a chance. Although challenging in every possible way, we grew so much spiritually, individually, and as a couple.

Halfway through the school was when everyone started to get really sick. Fatigue, lack of running water sometimes, and blistering heat seemed to be the perfect equation for sickness to breed. A few students found themselves sweating in their bunks with sickness, my husband Sam included. Sam became the sickest I had ever seen him. He developed such a strong form of bronchitis that his stomach was bleeding. On top of that, he had caught a staph infection from a soccer wound and was running a fever of 104 Fahrenheit. There we were in Africa! With Internet access being little or mostly extinct and phone calls back home rarely reaching, we were feeling pretty stretched and isolated to say the least!

The staff there was amazing, constantly coming to our hut and checking on him. Unfortunately, the medicine wasn't working, and his fever wasn't ceasing. "If he doesn't get better soon, you might have to go home," doctors pulled me aside and relayed to me. Reality then hit! It was then that I felt the danger and reality of the situation.

I remember going into the kitchen next to our room, just to escape the sight of my husband and sounds of him moaning. It was then that I cried out to God:

Lord. Where are You?! Here I am Lord! Remember me— your daughter. Why is this happening, God? We've seen countless people healed of diseases as we pray for them, and yet Sam keeps getting worse! We can't go home, God. That's not Your plan and I know it. That's just the enemy trying to discourage us. But Lord, I can't go on seeing him like this. God, where are You? Won't You come help?

It was then, at my breaking point after days of prayer and being unable to hear the Lord, that I heard Him. "Go and worship Me! Praise My name. Sing My name over him."

"OK, Lord," was my response, but honestly I was in disbelief that that would change the situation at all.

I went back into our room and sat on the bed next to my husband. "Sam, I'm gonna do something kind of weird, but Jesus told me to do it. He told me to lay my hands on you and just start praising His name, so that's what I am going to do, OK?"

"Mmmmm OK," he moaned back.

So I did exactly that. I placed my hands on his chest first. At this point, his entire body was soaked with sweat from the fever. I placed my hands on his chest and started singing out the name of Jesus. I just began to worship the Lord with my eyes closed and sing out His name. After about three minutes, something happened. His chest felt cooler! The fever was breaking! Next, I touched his forehead, which was still on fire. I did the same thing—praising the name of Jesus and singing Him worship songs over Sam. Slowly, the fever completely broke over his entire body!

This was a first for me, but I learned so much through that lesson with Holy Spirit. First, I was able to take my eyes off the sickness by just shutting them and singing to the Lord. Second, the power of praise shifts the atmosphere and loosens the enemy's grip over us! That day Sam's fever completely broke, and in a few days he regained his full strength.

Now I want to fast forward a couple of months to our experience in India. We were living in Calcutta, India and working as missionaries. It was in India that I truly learned to make war on the enemy! In Africa with the Bakers, we were constantly surrounded by witch doctors and demonic presence as we would go out and minister the gospel. However, there was a sweet covering being under the Bakers! They are seasoned missionaries who clearly know how to deal with assaults of the enemy. But it was in India, when we were on our own, that we really learned how to fight against spiritual warfare.

We were living in an area where there were Hindu temples all around us. In India, especially in Calcutta, the spiritual oppression is so prevalent and strong that you can feel it immediately as you get off the plane. The time that we spent there was one of the hardest on our marriage that we have ever experienced. Missions has a way of bringing out the worst and best in all of us as we are stretched beyond our limits in every way possible. Sam and I were constantly fighting, projecting our frustrations with day-to-day life there in Calcutta onto each other. We were quite isolated and were picking up all the warfare around us as we would do ministry.

It was there that, for the first time in my life, I couldn't hear God's voice. I would pray and ask Him questions, and it would feel like there was a glass ceiling there blocking my prayers from reaching Him and His answers from reaching me. (This is also another form of warfare we were against but didn't realize it at the time.) It was one of the loneliest and scariest feelings.

Friction causes sacrificial praise!

One day I went into a separate room, got down on my knees, and begged the Lord to speak to me and help me through all the tensions in our marriage. Suddenly, I found myself up in heaven. Call it what you will—an open vision, a closed vision, an encounter, whatever it was—I wasn't in that room anymore but in a completely different location. I walked down a large corridor with the Lord until we got to a specific door. Jesus took the handle in His hand, looked at me, smiled, and pushed it open.

I walked in and the door shut. I found myself completely alone in this new room but able to hear the Father speaking to me clearly. What I saw still to this day amazes me. All around the great room I saw armor of all different types. There were swords, axe-like tools with large handles, shoulder guards, wrist guards, guards of all different types. There were musical instruments—shofars, trumpets, harps, drums, etc. There were bows and arrows, helmets, breastplates, and swords. In one corner I saw huge, full-body suits that looked immensely strong in bronze and golden colors. I also saw special shoes that looked unbreakable but light as a feather. "Pick whatever you want, Ana," I heard the Father say. "This is My room of spiritual armor."

It was then that I saw angels come in and bustle all about the room. For some reason, I had the knowledge at that moment that they were picking armor out for the specific people they were assigned to bring them to.

I glanced back around the room and was drawn to all the strong, huge-looking armor. *Hmm,* I thought. *That's not a bad place to start!* As I approached the large armor, though, nothing really stuck out to me as my armor. So I started riffling through the armor.

There amidst the big bronze armor, I found mine. I don't know how to explain it, except that in the moment I just knew it was made for me. It was a beautiful and light-looking dress. Almost similar to the chainmail knights wore under their armor, except this one looked glorious. It glimmered in the light all the different colors of the rainbow and almost looked translucent. Along the edges of the dress, I was astonished as I saw all kinds of different pearls inlaid in the pattern. There was something enticing about the pearls; I just couldn't peel my eyes away from them.

"This, Ana, is the garment of praise," I heard the Lord say. "You have chosen well!" the Lord smiled back at me. I looked at Him questioningly. It was like He read my mind in that moment and answered the question that had been daunting me. "The pearls represent sacrificial praise—for all the times you will have to turn to praising Me, even when you don't feel like it, to break the enemy's hold."

I put on the garment, which felt amazingly light and warm, and just like that I was back in India—now with my face on the floor and tears running down from my eyes.

Pearls and Sacrificial Praise

I researched how pearls are formed after this experience with God and discovered something wild. Without boring you with too much scientific mumbo-jumbo, to summarize—pearls are created out of friction. When a muscle or mollusk feels threatened by a foreign object, it creates a pearl as a defense mechanism. It dawned on me—friction causes sacrificial praise!

It's one thing to praise God when our lives are going great—we receive a blessing, finances are flowing, and our family life and ministry is bearing fruit. But will we praise Him when this life is rough? Will we praise Him when we can't see beyond our own sorrow, problems, or pain? Will we even praise Him when we can't see the fruit of our labor?

Hebrews 13:15 says, "Through Him then, let us continually offer up a sacrifice of praise to God, that is, the fruit of lips that give thanks to His name" (NASB). Psalms 50:14 says, "Offer to God a sacrifice of thanksgiving and pay your vows to the Most High" (NASB).

I was looking up sacrifice in the dictionary the other day, and guess what it means? *Sacrifice!* It is an offering of something or a surrendering. Look it up! Go on, I dare you! It might actually hit you with revelation as it did me. So when the Scriptures talk about making an offering of sacrificial praise, it's referring to praising the King who is worthy of praise even when we don't feel like it and it's difficult. It's the simple act of saying,

"God, I will praise You even though I don't understand what is going on right now. I will surrender my trust to You. You are a good God, and You are so worthy of all my love and devotion, even right now amidst all of this chaos in my life! I set my eyes on You, Father! Thank You, God, for this chastening!"

Will we praise Him when this life is rough?

Why Praise

When he had consulted with the people, he appointed those who sang to the Lord and those who praised Him in holy attire, as they went out before the army and said, "Give thanks to the Lord, for His lovingkindness is everlasting." When they began singing and praising, the Lord set ambushes against the sons of Ammon, Moab and Mount Seir, who had come against Judah; so they were routed (2 Chronicles 20:21-22).

This specific scripture shows the power of praise. Jehoshaphat was in trouble. A group of men had rounded up a whole army to come fight against all of Judah and Jerusalem, so Jehoshaphat declared a fast throughout the nation to seek out the Lord's wisdom. Strategically, Jehoshaphat places the worshipers on the very front of the battlefield. Not the strongest warriors, but perhaps the strongest warriors in the spirit! They go out and start singing praise songs to the Lord, and then the Lord fights the battle for them. The key to look at here is the fact that they *go!* They engage in worship and then we see God responding. Worship, praise, and thanksgiving shifts the atmosphere in times of spiritual warfare.

Now I realize as I'm writing this some of you are thinking, *OK, easier said than done!* In all honesty, as I've been writing this chapter I've been hit with one spiritual warfare attack after another. It's like the enemy has been challenging me, "Do you really believe and do what you say to do in hard times?"

There are days when I don't feel like praising God at all because things feel so tough. There are days when, selfishly, I would rather focus on my problems than focus on Him. I have to come back though to what I know, and that is that *"God causes all things to work together for good to those who love God"* (Rom. 8:28 NASB). He is a good Father despite what I can see in front of me right now. Despite all my problems and all the spiritual warfare I am experiencing now, He is still worthy of all my praise. I have to trust Him!

Activation Prayer

God, I come to You now and confess my own lack of understanding. I am helplessly surrendered to You, Father, and it's a good place to be. I can't control my situation. All I can do is change my heart's attitude. It's hard, God, and You know where I am today as I am sitting here before You. I just pour out my heart to You because I know You care. I trust You, God. I choose now to just praise You and declare that I will not be overwhelmed! Your blood covers me and washes over me. I am Your beloved! Thank You, Father, for being a good Dad who takes care of me despite what I can see! Amen.

Application

Now spend some time praising Him. Go into your room, shut the door, and just begin praising Him. If you are struggling with this, just begin thanking Him. Thank Him as long as you can. Now go for a little more, and then begin to sing praise to Him. Sing whatever comes to mind or put on some worship music to sing along with. As silly as this might feel the first time you do it, remember you are shifting the atmosphere and God loves our praise! So take it seriously. Praise is weaponry!

Discussion Questions

1. What do you think your armor is? Besides praise, take time and ask the Lord to show you what armor He has specifically assigned to you.

Chapter 4

Making War Against
the Enemy

One night, I faced an increased amount of what I would call "spiritual warfare." Spiritual warfare can look different to each person, but to me this was war! My husband and I had just announced to his parents our return from missions in Nepal. At this time, we had been overseas working with Iris Ministries for a year and a half, first in Mozambique, Africa and then in India and Nepal. It's amazing how sometimes the enemy tries to strike right after we make steps out in faith. What's even more amazing is that I didn't see this coming. You would think that after dealing with warfare out in the mission field, I would be an expert at how to fight against it by now, but nope! We made our announcement, and then it showered down. At first I didn't even think, *Hey this is warfare! Maybe we should start to pray!* Instead, I was bombarded by thoughts of doubt. My faith was decreasing rapidly.

What if people don't understand our transition from missions right now? What if people don't understand that we are not leaving ministry and that it is just morphing into something different for us? What if we completely lose our support even though we are following God? What then, God? Why, God, are You calling us to leave Nepal and head back to Kansas City? What if we'll be up against a closed door for us there? What if nothing opens like You say it will, God? God, can't You start opening things now so that we really know that You're in this? The fear ran deeper and deeper in me as all these thoughts kept flooding my mind. Sometimes the hardest and largest battle zone can be in our own minds.

So we went to sleep—sort of. I woke up about two hours later to the hot breath of something breathing on my face. It smelled repulsive! At first I wanted to toss a pillow at my husband, thinking, *Can that really be him breathing on me?* Then my hair stood up on the back of my neck as I realized the hot breath was coming from the other side of the room. *It's something else! Eek*, I thought. I opened my eyes, and there he was. I like to call this demon my Ogre of Discouragement. I have never seen something quite like him, and this wasn't the first time I'd seen a demon. He was from floor to ceiling in height and about five times my width. Now, maybe you're thinking here, *That's not so bad.* Let me assure you, if you wake up to anything of that size, repulsive smell, and scary-looking build with red eyes glaring at you—yep, that's bad! Just about when

I felt like I wanted to scream, I heard Holy Spirit say, "It's time to war!"

Sometimes the hardest and largest battle zone can be in our own minds.

Making War

Even though I felt so terrified that I was forgetting to breathe, I went out of the bedroom, into the living room with the demonic presence following closely behind me, and I shut the door. With my eyes shut, filled with terror, I began to praise the Lord. I began singing whatever worship songs would come to my mind. Then I began to just thank Him for the amazing things He had done in my life. "I will praise You despite my fear. I will rise to this challenge. The enemy can never and will never tear my love and devotion to You, no matter the cost!" I found myself saying.

Something amazing happened. At first when I started to sing worship songs, the demonic presence grew more intense and came closer to me. My fear intensified, but I kept praising the Lord. The demon started to shriek, then said things to me like, "You'll always be alone. God will not take care of you. Are you sure God really loves you?" That's when I knew God and I were winning the battle. When the enemy desperately increases the attack, there is breakthrough coming just around the corner. So rather than agree with that discouraging voice, it only fueled my fire of love and desire to praise the Lord more.

Something interesting and totally amazing happened then. Just like a balloon letting out its air, this big demonic ogre began to shrink in size and width. The more I praised God and cried out to Him, the more the demonic presence lost his power or authority to be there. As I repented for ever agreeing with fear, discouragement, or doubt, I saw my sword, the one the Lord had given me in Africa, shine right in front of my face. "Thank You, Holy Spirit!" I cried out. I grabbed my sword, which was hot, and continued to praise the Lord.

Then something shifted in the atmosphere, and I felt faith arise in me to start making prophetic declarations. I began saying back the promises I had heard from the Father over my life and my husband's. "I praise You, Father, that I will never be alone. You go before me and are behind me always. You have prepared a way for our future. Thank You that you have said You will always take care of us, that we will always have enough, that as we lavishly give our lives to serve You, You will lavishly love upon us and bless us. God, I just want to spend my life washing Your feet. Nothing can separate my love and devotion to You! Thank You that You have promised us that our children will be blessed. Thank You that You are calling us back to the International House of Prayer. Thank You that there will be a role for us and direction for us there. Thank You that we will find support there. I prophetically declare now, in the name of Jesus, that fear and discouragement must leave this house now!"

As I said all this, my sword grew larger and hotter. As it grew hotter in my hand, the demonic presence grew smaller and smaller. Finally, when my sword was so hot that I could barely hold on to it without burning my hand, I took it and stabbed that demon! "You must leave now in the name of Jesus and not come back!" I yelled. Guess what! It did. Immediately, the battle was over. That demonic presence retreated out our front door knowing it had been defeated.

When the enemy desperately increases the attack, there is breakthrough coming just around the corner.

Replenished

Then the most glorious thing happened. There in my little living room, a glory cloud came. What did it look like? It was a thick cloud that filled the room completely. Flashes of colors moved through it, looking almost like a moving body of water. It seemed like the cloud was alive. Gold, purple, hues of blue, crimson red were mostly the colors I saw. There were also colors I cannot even describe. I've never seen them here on earth. The living presence of God was so thick that I just fell down, face flat on the floor. All I could say through tears was just, "I love You, Lord! I love You, Lord." It brought a whole new meaning of "the fear of the Lord."

Then the most marvelous and odd thing happened. The cloud began to speak back. I heard a song from the Father. "How I love you. My daughter, how proud I am of you. I am always with you, and I am preparing the way for you. You will always carry My presence wherever you go, for I am with you." Then He went on to sing to me more promises for my future.

As I cried out to the Father how much I loved Him in that moment, He would sing back His love over me!

This circle continued and continued for what seemed like hours; then suddenly, it just stopped. The cloud was gone, and I got off the floor. Before I had felt completely exhausted from my previous battle, but now I felt completely replenished, energized, and full from the glorious presence of the Father. My husband woke up the next morning, and as I told him everything that had happened and all the future promises the Lord had said, angelic presence filled our living room. My husband is not a seer but is incredibly prophetic and carries a strong gift of discernment. So there we sat in complete silence and awe of God as Sam felt the presence of the Lord and I watched the angels dancing throughout our room. Afterward, we praised the Lord for His goodness and faithfulness to us.

The living presence of God was so thick

that I just fell down, face flat on the floor.

All I could say through tears was just,

"I love You, Lord! I love You, Lord."

Why Prophetic Declarations Work

James 3:10 says "*Out of the same mouth proceed blessing and cursing*" (NKJV). Also in Luke 6:45 it says, "*For out of the abundance of the heart his mouth speaks*" (NKJV). We as believers, who have the living Christ dwelling inside of us, have so much power and authority in our tongue. That's why God takes it very seriously when we sinfully curse another, speak harshly, or gossip. Likewise, we have the power to unleash promises of God over ourselves or unleash negativity and fear.

I once met this woman who would constantly make statements to me like, "Just pray for me that my doctor's appointment doesn't go bad," or "Just pray for me that the family dinner won't be a disaster." It took me years to pinpoint exactly what bothered me about this lady's prayer requests. She was speaking forth the negative without even realizing it, instead of making statements like, "Pray for me that my doctor appointment will be excellent," or "Pray that my family get together will be a wonderful experience." Do you see the difference? It's like she was already agreeing with the enemy that the outcomes would be negative.

This is why it is so important that as we face our battles our mind-sets are first renewed by the thoughts of Christ. When I recognized that my thoughts and emotions were not aligned with the Lord's thoughts and emotions, I battled that demon by first entering into His presence through praise and worship and then started declaring the promises of God. This is a great way to get your thoughts and emotions transformed even when it doesn't come naturally. Then, as I began to declare these truths out loud, I noticed that the attack of fear and discouragement began to quickly dissipate. I took on the thoughts of Christ, and everything else had to leave!

Revelation 19:10 says, *"It is the Spirit of prophecy who bears testimony to Jesus"* (NIV). It always amazes me to watch how, when people share their healing testimonies, other people in the same room who need that same miracle get touched by God and receive healing. There is power when we align our tongue with heaven and what the Father says, thinks, and wants to do.

Making prophetic declarations also activates faith. It is declaring what is unseen into possibility. If anyone has heard me speak, they quickly learn that one of my favorite scriptures is 1 Samuel 17:45-47. David is about to fight Goliath, and with all odds against him he declares *"This day the Lord will deliver you into my hands, and I'll strike you down and cut off your head. ... For the battle is the Lord's, and He will give all of you into our hands"* (NIV). Talk about facing your enemy! As David makes this prophetic declaration, he is taking up the posture of a victorious one, not a defeated one.

This scripture shows David partnering with Heaven. In a sense he is saying, "My God is bigger, and you don't stand a chance buddy!" John 10:10 says, *"The thief comes only to steal and kill and destroy; I have come that they may have life, and have it to the full"* (NIV). Isn't it nice to know that as we prophetically declare what the Lord has shown us, we are agreeing with the Father on our own behalf? He wants us to have life and not live under the accusations and oppression of the accuser. We shift the atmosphere of the battlefield by agreeing with the Father through our declarations, and we put the enemy in the position of retreat.

We enter into His very presence through our unreserved worship, praise, and thanksgiving.

Prophetic declarations also change our perspective into a heavenly one. As I fought that demonic presence and began to declare the promises the Lord had spoken over my husband

and me, I could see the enemy losing his power and shrinking. What seemed so scary at first became actually rather small and easy to conquer. *"I can do all things through Christ who strengthens me"* (Phil. 4:13 NKJV).

Entering His Gates

Psalms 100:4 says, *"Enter his gates with thanksgiving and his courts with praise; give thanks to him and praise his name"* (NIV). I've already written in Chapter 3 of this book about praise, but I feel it necessary here to reemphasize a few points. When I faced that demonic presence, what defueled its authority to be there was my praise and thanksgiving to the Lord. As soon as I started praising the Lord, the demonic presence had to shrink. We enter into His very presence through our unreserved worship, praise, and thanksgiving.

Activation

Step 1

If you are finding yourself in a battle right now, no matter the size, ask the Lord to show you what you might be up against. Ephesians 6:12 says, *"For our struggle is not against flesh and blood, but against the rulers, against the authorities, against the powers of this dark world and against the spiritual forces of evil in the heavenly realms."* Not everything is a spiritual battle! Some struggles we bring upon ourselves through our own free will and sinful nature. Ask yourself this right now: *This situation I am in right now that is proving to be difficult—could it be warfare or something else?* If this struggle is something you could be going through because the Lord is chastening you and equipping you through it, *praise* the Lord! He's training you! If it is a struggle you've brought on yourself, meet with someone in the church you know and trust to carry wisdom, and repent and get clean from whatever sin you need to. We are all unclean vessels struggling to keep our hearts pure before the Lord, so don't allow yourself to feel shame in asking for help.

If it is warfare, ask yourself, "Are any of my emotions right now different than the fruits of the Spirit—love, joy, peace, patience, kindness, goodness, faithfulness, gentleness, and self-control (see Gal. 5:22) or outside of Christ's nature?" This might help pinpoint demonic activity that is present. A few examples of this are fear, depression, self-hatred, jealousy, defeat, anxiety, offense.

Last, ask yourself, "Is there any lie I am believing here?" If there is one, God will reveal it. If you don't hear anything, don't press it until you hear something.

> *Lord, I pray that You would reveal if there is any demonic activity involved right now for the person reading this. Holy Spirit, come. Are there any lies that have been believed that are fueling the enemy's power? Lord, thank You that we as believers are cleansed in Your blood. Thank You for whatever You have revealed right now to the reader, and thank You that You have power over every demonic activity or principality.*

Step 2

As you prayed through step 1 of the activation, don't feel discouraged if you didn't hear anything! Move on to step 3 then.

If Holy Spirit did reveal anything to you in step 1, then get ready to do some battle! Ephesians 6:14-17 says, *"Stand firm then, with the belt of truth buckled around your waist, with the breastplate of righteousness in place, and with your feet fitted with the readiness that comes from the gospel of peace. In addition to all this, take up the shield of faith, with which you can extinguish all the flaming arrows of the evil one. Take the helmet of salvation and the sword of the Spirit, which is the word of God."* Go ahead and walk yourself through putting on your spiritual armor. If you've never done this before, sometimes it helps me to say, "I put to my belt of truth," etc. to visually help me engage with the Lord in the act of putting on my armor.

Step 3

Now go ahead and move into a time of worship, praise, and thanking the Lord. If the Lord hasn't gifted you with a great singing voice or hands that play an instrument, that's OK. Put on some worship music and worship at the top of your lungs anyway! God loves it! Start giving thanks to the Lord for His goodness and all that He has done for you.

Step 4

Now, once you start to sense the presence of the Lord in the room, start to make declarations counter to what you are up against, which you discovered in step 1. Speak out the promises that God has shown you about your life. Now, maybe you're thinking, *But I don't know the promises God has for my life!* Well, this might be a good time to start asking Him. As you hear the Lord speak them to you, start declaring them out. A simple, practical way to do this is, "God thank You that You have shown me and told me _____." Keep making as many declarations as you can, and even say them a few times to dismantle the enemy's power. If there is a lie you discovered that you may have been believing, ask the Lord to reveal to you truth, and then begin declaring that out.

If you don't feel a shift happening, call on the name of Jesus to come help you. Keep doing steps 3 and 4 until you feel a shift happen. If you are sensitive to Holy Spirit, you might feel a literal shift in the atmosphere. If you are a seer, you might see that demon shrink and leave. If you love the Lord, a shift might look like feeling encouraged, a change until you are not feeling those arrows of the enemy that you were feeling in step 1.

Activation Prayer

Lord, I seal everything that You have done here today in the blood of Christ. Father, I ask You to place a seal of protection around them and close any back door that the enemy might try and sneak back in through. Thank You, Father, for breakthrough! Amen.

Discussion Questions

1. What declarations do you want to make over yourself this week?

2. How can you keep yourself accountable to make them?

3. Where can you place them so you have a visual reminder?

Chapter 5

Sitting at the Father's Table

Once, I was invited up to the Father's table. I was sitting in a worship set in the prayer room at International House of Prayer when suddenly I heard Holy Spirit's voice. "Come up here, I want to give you something!" I shut my eyes and suddenly saw a strong vision.

There I was in a large room. The room seemed to be endless, full of activity, and glowing with warmth. There was Jesus, sitting down at a huge table. I'll never forget His face in that moment! He was so full of joy; invitation and acceptance were in his eyes, and He seemed to be bubbling with laughter.

"Come sit down," He said. I sat down and then began to take in the scrumptious display before me. The table was laid bountifully with a multitude of food. Many of the foods I did not recognize. There were new fruits of bright colors. On the table lay a few choice foods that I loved, and my eyes lit up with excitement. Looking at me, Jesus laughed and said "Take and eat whatever you desire." So I did! I filled my plate with all kinds of different varieties of delicious foods and ate with Jesus. He slurped on a bowl of soup. Looking back on this vision, I just have to laugh. To think that the majestic and glorious God Himself would take the time to humbly slurp soup with me! It just makes me realize more and more how deep His love runs for me.

After I ate a little, I looked at Jesus sheepishly and wanted to ask, "So, Lord, why I am here?" but feeling embarrassed and still in shock that I was eating with Jesus, I said nothing.

He laughed back at me with excitement and a twinkle in his eyes and said, "I thought you would never ask! I want to show you something." That's when the reality hit me that God is all-knowing and that He knows my innermost thoughts.

I then noticed before me a huge golden bowl filled to the brim with pomegranates. I don't know why I hadn't noticed it before. Perhaps my eyes were blind to it before. I looked at Jesus a little perplexed. Pomegranates have always been my favorite fruit and smell. "Are those for me?" I asked.

"Of course," he laughed joyously back. "I want you to look up pomegranates in the Bible. See, they were for the royal. For those who knew their royalty." So, I took one and bit into it. It was the most delicious pomegranate I have ever tasted in my life. Eating in heaven is divine!

As I was thoroughly enjoying myself eating my pomegranate, suddenly I heard movement coming from under the table. "Lord, what's that?" I thought.

Immediately, I heard him respond back, "Come have a look with me." It's odd to describe, but many times during my heaven encounters people just seem to communicate without ever opening their mouths. I guess everything is just laid bare and transparent, so there's often no need for words.

I got off my chair and so did Jesus. We went to crawl down under the table. Suddenly, I was looking at the most horrific sight. I was standing with the Lord before a barren land. Malnourished looking people were scrounging around on the dirt floor, searching in desperation for crumbs. They were barely surviving. I could see that a survivor mentality had set in, and each person barely even recognized the other people around them. Then, just as sudden as it was when I was taken up in this vision, I was back in the prayer room. A whole hour and a half had passed. I've experienced this before—often heaven's time is different from earthly time.

I will never forget the experience above and below the table that day. Those poor people who were scavenging for the Father's crumbs didn't know what scrumptious food was available to them. They were living under a broken identity and understanding of the Father's love. How wonderful it is to know His heart. By knowing His heart we step into the realization and acceptance that His heart is for us! It's time for the body of Christ to break away from the degradation of who God has made us to be.

I have sat with many believers who at their core have believed a lie that they are not good enough. They see the world through a lens of inferiority and don't even realize it. If we look back to satan falling from heaven (see Isa. 14:12-15), we can observe that jealousy and comparison were two of the main sins ruling lucifer's heart. If we fall into the trap of comparing with others' abilities or thinking less of ourselves than the way the Lord sees us, we are playing with fire. That fire is fueled and comes from hell. Literally! Satan comes to steal us from walking in the fullness of Christ (see John 10:10). Walking in the fullness of Christ means walking in our own identities. The Creator of heaven and earth created you to be unique and desires for you to walk in who He made you to be. No more trying to put on others' mantles. Just start walking in your own. If we are trying to mirror someone else's gifting or are stuck falling up short because we are always comparing ourselves to others, we have fallen into the trap of satan.

Maturity comes with proper nourishment. To have a healthy diet, they must know their identity in Me,

The encounter I had in heaven revealed not only the state some believers are in today but also the very nature of Christ—to pull us up from under the table and crown us with honor and with a place at the Father's table. The second part of John 10:10 says, "*I have come that they may have life, and have it to the full*" (NIV).

I work with this group of youth who are between the ages of ten and fifteen. The neighborhood they live in is poor, full of violence and drug dealing. Just this past week, a group of us leaders spent time talking to the kids about their royalty in

Christ. We asked them how they would change their neighborhood if they were the Queen or King of it. Slowly but surely, we are working to instill in them their value in the Lord. Every day they get bombarded with defeat, put-downs, and lies from the rest of their world. Every time they come to Bible study, we try to treat them and teach them according to their value and royalty in Jesus. Last week after our meeting, I actually witnessed the kids trying on fake crowns we had. Sometimes, I wonder if they are listening! It's a battle just to get them to put away their phones for 10 minutes and listen. I know, though, that something from last week had sunk in.

After my encounter at the Father's table, I went and researched pomegranates in the Bible. I found in Exodus 39:24-26 that pomegranates were sewn into the hems of the robes that the priests wore when ministering in the sanctuary of Moses' tabernacle. I got the message! I heard later, "Enter in, knowing that you are royal! No longer can you settle for just the crumbs. You have a responsibility to sit at this table and partake in the Father's goodness and pleasure for you. Also, you have a responsibility to bring others up here. Gather My children who are starving because they don't know. Then don't know how pleased I am with them! I want them to eat my solid food. I want them to mature! Maturity comes with proper nourishment. To have a healthy diet, they must know their identity in Me, which comes from eating from this table I've set before you."

I don't know if you've ever seen what a malnourished person looks like, but in all my travels overseas I have seen quite a few examples of malnourishment. In Africa especially, when my husband and I worked with Iris Ministries, we would go out to far, remote villages to preach the gospel. There we would see children with huge, bloated bellies. We saw this in the streets of India too. Bloated bellies are one of the sure signs of malnourishment. The bellies look full, but they are swollen because of the lack of good nutrition and being filled with foods that just leave them starving. Often, it's also a sign of parasites. Think about how this relates to what I saw under the Father's table! I saw people starving, with similar bloated bellies, fighting for just the leftover crumbs. Those tummies were getting full with other substances that were not of nutritional value but just a temporary fix for their hunger pains.

As I read deeper into Scripture about the priestly roles and duties, I became intrigued. In the Word, it says that the priest would have a lottery to see who would get to enter into the very temple of the Lord and make an offering of incense (see Luke 1:9). Of all the priestly duties, that's where I'd want to be! I'd want to be the one chosen who gets to enter into His very presence. Oh, what that would be like! Can you just imagine? It would be like winning the ultimate and only lottery worth winning!

Matthew 27:51 shows us that the veil was torn. That very presence, which only one chosen priest a year could experience, was let loose that day when Jesus took back the keys of hell from the enemy. Often, it's easy to look past the power behind Jesus' resurrection from the cross. It's our very hope!

We are living now under a new covenant. Jesus made a way for us to enter in. What a contrast between the Old Testament picture—only one priest being able to experience His presence—and the disciples getting to take communion with the living God. Even more so is the vision I had where Jesus

Himself invited me to sit with Him at His table and experience His pleasure over me. *"But you, Lord, are a shield around me, my glory, the One who lifts my head high"* (Ps. 3:3 NIV).

Activation

Let's go back to the Father's table. Can you see yourself sitting there? Right now, pray and ask Holy Spirit to come. Try to quiet down your mind. Remove anything that might distract you from the room. I recommend going to the Father's table in a room where you can shut the door and shut out outside noises. Play worship music gently in the background if this helps you enter into His presence. Meditate on the scripture, *"You prepare a table before me in the presence of my enemies"* (Ps. 23:5 NIV). Now try and see a picture of what being at that table would look like. Are you there?

> *Holy Spirit, I pray and I ask You to come fill this reader's room right now. Lord, lead them up to Your table. I speak and pray against any warfare that may come to distract or discourage them from being able to receive visions from You. Thank You, Father, that visions of heaven are for all of us. I pray that You would enter into this time, Lord, and put an angelic wall of defense up around anything else entering into this vision or time that is not from You. Thank You, Abba. Amen*

If you haven't been able to see a clear vision of the Father's table yet, don't get discouraged. Receiving visions from the Lord is truly a gift, and sometimes it takes time and practice.

Whether or not you can see yourself at the Father's table, where do you picture yourself? Are you under the table or sitting at it?

The Lord has given you authority to cast out demonic oppression.

Under the Table: Activation

First off, if you find yourself underneath the Father's table and find yourself relating to the vision God gave me of the malnourished and starving church of today, don't feel ashamed. God desperately wants to bring you up to a new level.

If you find yourself relating to the words I wrote earlier— always feeling like you come up short when you compare yourself to other people—I have a specific prayer for you. This self-belittling inferiority complex has to stop now! This literally is the enemy trying to rob you of your own destiny and royal identity that the Lord has given you. The Lord takes serious offense to His bride thinking less of herself and moving in jealousy toward others. Breaking this comparison cycle starts first with self-acceptance. If, as you're reading this, the word *self-acceptance* resonates with you at all, even if you don't understand why yet, and you are realizing that you need a deeper level of it (as I think we all do at times), go ahead and read the following prayer out loud if you can.

Lord. Here I am, God. Father, I need more of You. I need to know Your love for me deeper so that I may love myself better. I'm sorry, Lord, for sometimes comparing myself to other people or thinking less of myself than the way you see me. Father, today I just choose to say—I love myself. I love the way You made me. I love and cherish everything about the way I am. I am like no one else, and that makes me special. Today I just choose to embrace the way I am. Forgive me, Lord, for falling into the sin of comparison. Please come and wash me clean of this pattern. I also renounce any area of self-rejection. I renounce any bit of self-hatred I've felt. I also renounce being too critical of myself sometimes. Lord, please show me if there are any roots to these issues. (Pause here and wait on Holy Spirit to reveal anything to you if there are roots.) God, reveal Your truth and light in each of these situations. Help me rip out any of these roots. Today I choose to walk in light, in love for myself, and in freedom from comparison. Amen.

As I am writing this, I have a picture that I think is from the Lord for some of the readers. I see a vision of a little bird with its wings tied down. Years of being restrained have made you discredit yourself and your own abilities. This is causing you to think that you don't belong at the Father's table. That is such a lie!

I also hear that someone reading this has experienced years of having their voice oppressed. If that's you, place your hand over your throat. The Lord has given you authority to cast out demonic oppression. *"I have given you authority to trample on snakes and scorpions and to overcome all the power of the enemy"* (Luke 10:19 NIV). Say:

I rebuke the enemy's hand; it cannot be on me any longer in the name of Jesus. I call out my own voice now and say it's time to be heard. The Lord has given me a sound mind, a strong voice, and a powerful testimony that needs to be heard! I renounced any lies I have come to believe about being powerless. God, show me if there are any other lies I need to renounce now. (Pause here and ask Holy Spirit to reveal anything.) Thank You, Father. Amen.

Guilt is also a strong way the oppressor can keep us from fully receiving the goodness of God. Repentance is a wonderful thing, and it is also biblical. *"I tell you that in the same way there will be more rejoicing in heaven over one sinner who repents than over ninety-nine righteous persons who do not need to repent"* (Luke 15:7 NIV). To repent means to admit your wrongs, ask for forgiveness, and then to literally turn away from the sin and not keep looking back at it with guilt or shame. You are not the judge! Someone reading this needs to say *"Amen!"* after reading that! I'm serious! You are not the judge. Right now, if you find yourself struggling with self-condemnation or realizing that you tend to be critical of others, renounce a critical spirit.

Thank You, Father, that You are my Judge. Father, one day we will each have to stand before You in all Your holiness, perfection, and pureness, and You will judge us each individually. Thank You that You give me grace, Lord. Father, thank You that Jesus has paid the price for me. Forgive me, Father, for ＿＿＿＿＿＿＿＿. Today, I choose to receive Your forgiveness and choose to forgive myself. Now I'm going to walk in freedom from this sin and the power it's had in my life. Your Word says that Your blood has cleansed me from my sins. I receive Your forgiveness and what you did for me on the cross (see Heb. 10:22). I choose to stand in this today. Amen.

Finally, I hear that someone reading this right now has been overlooked in ministry. You've humbly served for years in a position that does not draw attention to yourself, nor do you receive promotion from others for it. Perhaps it's being an intercessor in a prayer closet or somewhere hidden from the people's attention. Health issues or family issues may have kept you there. I have great news for you! Jesus wasn't released into His ministry until He was thirty; He had a ministry that lasted for only three years but radically changed the world forever! Don't discredit yourself because you haven't been released yet into the ministry that you know is coming. Come on! Hang on to His promises! You, who have spent so much time hanging out with the Beloved, must know that your position is to sit at the table and dine with the King.

I met this little 80-year-old lady once at Bethel Church. For years she sat in the place of intercession for countless people in her house. She truly was an Anna (see Luke 2:36-38). As I met her, the Lord shared with me, "This little lady has done more for Me in her rocker than you have done in your short time in ministry. Don't discredit her, because she is one of My precious gems." Don't ever limit, discredit, or think less of yourself, for these are the plans of the enemy.

Sitting at Our Rightful Place

Are we there now? Can you imagine yourself sitting at the Father's table? Now if you can envision Jesus sitting there, what do you see in His eyes when He looks at you? If you see anything that counters love, acceptance, gentleness, goodness, warmth—such as condemnation, anger, sadness, disappointment—please ask Holy Spirit to reveal to you why you are seeing or feeling this.

Sometimes, the revelation of sin in our lives might cause us to see the Father's eyes looking at us this way. At this point, before reading further you might need to take some time to do some heart examination and repent and come clean before the Father.

Also, there may be a separation in your relationship with the Father. Our own broken relationships with our earthly fathers can do this, or perhaps a broken relationship with a person who held authority in your life. Our own undealt-with pain can sometimes lead us to project it into our relationship with the Lord. Before you go digging into a journey of inner healing, ask the Holy Spirit to reveal to you what still needs to come to the surface and be healed. There's no need to keep going over and over the same things that you have already received breakthrough on. I pray that, as the Lord reveals areas to you that need His healing touch, you can stay in a place of feeling the goodness and pleasure of the Father for you.

Heavenly Room: Goodness and Pleasure

One day, I experienced walking through a part of heaven with Jesus. I am in no way claiming to be an expert on heaven, nor am I claiming to have seen it all. Being allowed to see portions of it, though, have made me definitely curious and craving to see more!

In a vision, the Lord approached me one day. "Come with Me. I want to show you something new." Just as simply as that, suddenly I found myself walking down a long hallway with Jesus. There were many different rooms I saw. Angels also bustled about joyfully, worshiping as they went about their tasks.

We came to a closed door, and immediately my heart started to pound and I felt my face get really hot. I was hit with fear and anticipation. *What is behind that door?* I thought. Jesus opened the door for me, but didn't enter in behind me. The realization that I had to face whatever was behind that door alone made me feel even more nervous.

> "You are more comfortable sitting in a glory
> cloud and experiencing the power and might
> of My character than you are with being
> here and experiencing the depth of My love
> and joy I feel over you. It's time for your
> old, rejected self to be washed anew."

Suddenly, I was blinded by such bright light. It's all I could really make out. My skin felt warmth on it too. As my eyes adjusted to the light, I was able to glance around the room, and something caught my attention. Besides the door where I had entered, the room seemed endless and without boundaries. I could see nothing that defined the edges of the room. I was intrigued by something else I saw, though. It looked like a flowing river mixed with vapor. It radiated colors that were like no colors I have ever seen on earth. Whatever it was, it was alive and moving and coming quickly toward me. I anticipated what would happen if it touched me. Suddenly, the river/vapor, turned sharply and passed right through me. As it passed through me, I felt the most amazing rush. I felt warmth, joy, peace, and a tangible love.

Then He spoke. I couldn't see Him, but His voice was unmistakable. "That's Holy Spirit. This is the room of my goodness and pleasure! It's here I've brought you to be filled in My love and feel the pride I feel for you. Don't you know how proud I am of you? Ana, you are more comfortable sitting in a glory cloud and experiencing the power and might of My character than you are with being here and experiencing the depth of My love and joy I feel over you. It's time for your old, rejected self to be washed anew."

I felt wave after wave of His love and pleasure wash over me. It was so strong; I couldn't do anything to resist it but just submit to its current. The current of God—ah, it's so wonderful! Finally, after what seemed like hours of being here, Jesus suddenly appeared beside me. "It's time to go now," He said and smiled back at me.

"Can I..." but I couldn't seem to get the words out. The question seemed stupid to ask at the moment.

"Yes, of course you can come back here!" He lovingly laughed and responded to me. "As often as you like!" And suddenly the vision was over. I was sitting back in my bedroom. Nothing had changed or been moved—except for me, of course! The Lord has graciously allowed me to go back to this room many times, whenever I need a refreshing touch.

Maintaining that refreshed feeling after leaving that room is the challenge. We live in such a broken world with broken people and also so many things to distract us from what we truly seek and need—the Father's love. This is what I mean by "try to stay in that place of feeling the goodness and pleasure of the Father for you." The enemy's number-one strategy is to steal our security in the love of the Father.

Activation: At the Father's Table

If you are able to see yourself now sitting at the table with the Father, can you feel the Lord's love, warmth, happiness, and delight over you? What can you see on the table? Between the Lord and me, pomegranates became my special food. At random times during meetings or during times of speaking, I would see in the spiritual realm pomegranates in the room. It was like a sweet, secret way for the Father to remind me of my royalty in Him.

The enemy's number-one strategy is to steal our security in the love of the Father.

What is the food you see? For different seasons, the Lord has also brought me to the table to eat different foods that always had a lesson tied with them for me at the time. I've spoken with other friends of mine who have shared with me that they too have had the similar experience of going to the Father's table and being offered different, special kinds of food. If God presents you a food that you've never seen before, research it. See if you can find out where it may grow, the germination pattern of it, and what it may be used for.

Often, though, the food I've seen is unearthly, and then I just have to ask the Lord to give me revelation about what He is trying to teach me through it.

As you grow more accustomed to eating from the Father's table, you can try looking around the room as you are with Him and see what else there is! You might be able to ask Him questions about other things He may reveal to you. God wants to raise up His bride who is confident in her position at His table!

Discussion Questions

1 Where do you see yourself seated at the Father's table? Are you sitting at it or under it?

2. What area of your life has the enemy recently been trying to steal your identity in?

3. Do you have a hard time receiving love, joy, or acceptance? Why do you think that is?

Chapter 6

Open and Closed Visions

People ask me all the time what it is like to see angels. Often people will come up to me who know I am a seer and put me on the spot, saying, "What do you see right now?" Sometimes in those moments I will have a picture for them or see something in the spiritual realm, but often for me it doesn't work like that. It would be like the equivalent of someone coming up to you in the grocery store line, saying, "What do you hear from God right now?" Granted, we should be a people who can prophesy on the spot like that, but I do believe it takes being in a certain mind-set or focusing in with the Lord to hear from Him or see with Him. That's the ultimate goal for every believer, though— to be so in tune with the Lord that we are constantly hearing and in touch with what is on His mind no matter where we are.

Also, quite often seers will see something, but they aren't released to share it now. Some visions are for the future or maybe even just keys for helping us minister, not meant for public knowledge. There are those moments, though, when I'll be doing something and at random catch a glimpse of something in the Spirit on someone and feel released to share.

One day, I was outside of the International House of Prayer just finishing up a conversation with my mom on the phone. My friend Sean came out of the prayer room just then, and randomly I saw in an open vision (just like I could see the next person in front of me) a monkey sitting on his shoulder, picking furiously at his hair. "Hold on one second, Mom," I said. "Hey Sean! You've got a monkey sitting on your shoulder, and I get the impression he's here to pester you. He's not a good monkey. Are you by any chance experiencing any sort of backlash right now?"

"In fact, I am!" he said. "I just got back from a ministry trip that was real rough, and I've been sick ever since I got back with a head cold." So I prayed for him then.

I would describe this vision as an open vision with God. Open visions are seeing something in the spiritual realm with your eyes open. It is just as if you can see that person sitting right across the room from you. Plain as day, I'll see an angel walk in the room. Sometimes open visions also will seem like a movie screen where a whole scene is just flashed on display right there in the middle of wherever you are.

Other visions can be closed visions, or seeing in your mind's eye. This may be like an impression or picture you get from the Lord while praying for someone. In a time of prayer or meditating on the Lord, He'll give you a picture that you can see with your eyes closed. Sometimes, I think it is easier to start walking in the seer anointing by asking the Lord for closed visions. That way you can close your eyes, shut off all other distractions, and focus on Him.

One time, I was ministering to a lady at Bethel Church in Redding, California. She had come to the healing conference that weekend, and I was on a team doing healing ministry. Now this is a very rare account, but it is a very good example of a closed vision. Our team prayed and prayed for her healing, and in all honesty we weren't getting any breakthrough. I decided to lay hands on her and ask the Lord why she wasn't getting freedom. Instantly, with my eyes closed I saw a picture of the woman, except I saw her as a young child. I saw a picture of a child cowering in a corner as an angry man approached her. I didn't see the exact interaction of the abuse, but it was enough to greatly disturb me.

Now this was one of those instances when I had to really ask the Lord, *Am I free to talk to her about this, Lord?* I was treading on dangerous waters. If the lady wasn't ready to face this, I surely didn't want to stir up the past and bring her more pain. So I waited. I waited on the Lord, and finally I heard Him say, "Just ask." So I asked her if there had ever been an instance of abuse in her childhood from an older man, and I apologized ahead of time just in case I was hearing this wrong from the Lord. Instantly, tears and sobbing started to erupt from the lady. She told us her story, and our team was able to minister inner healing to the lady. After we got done walking her through some grieving, forgiveness, and asking the Lord to replace some of the pain with new truths, the lady's physical affliction lifted.

Just like that she was physically healed! Often, I've found that inner healing releases breakthrough for the physical problems we are experiencing.

God also speaks to us through our dream life. It's very similar to a closed vision, but we are in a dream like state. I have had countless times when I've woken up from a dream thinking, *Man, what was that about?* I write down all my dreams, though, so I can revisit them later. Truthfully, not all dreams are from God, but in reality some are!

It takes hunger, appetite for Him, and curiosity for the seer realm to be released!

Once, I had a strong recurring dream. (If you start having a recurring dream or theme to your dreams—pay attention to it! God may be trying really hard to get your attention.) I had a dream that I was on a train ride. Suddenly, the train veered off the normal track and started speeding up at a dangerous rate. People in the train started panicking and screaming like crazy. In that moment, I had the fearful feeling of desperately needing to get off this train. Then, suddenly the train slowed down enough to where I could jump off onto a platform it passed along the way. A group of us jumped off to safety, and then the train started speeding up and took off again at a chaotic pace. The group of us climbed up a grassy hill to a park we found to sit down. We sat in the most gorgeous park; it had lush, green, rolling hills. There we ate and rested a bit from our crazy adventure. The girl sitting next to me who had crazy hair—who I now know represented Holy Spirit—then said to me, "OK. I think it's time for us to go now. That's where you'll find your ministry next." She pointed across the distance to a city far away where I could see lights from a night skyline. The place she was pointing to was clearly in a different time zone. We climbed the hill and left.

When I woke up from that dream, at the time I had no idea what God meant by it. It started to recur over the course of six months, so I knew it was important for me to understand. Later on, we were in India ministering to street children at a place where there were lots of trains. We were in a totally chaotic environment, and this dream helped us agree with God to go to Nepal and jump off that train. A ministry opportunity opened for us, so blindly but trusting in the Lord, we went to Nepal. When we drove up to our living quarters, to our shock we were overlooking the most gorgeous rolling hills of lush, green rice fields. Just like the grass hill in my dream, they literally surrounded our house! We stayed in Nepal for four and a half months until God eventually led us back to Kansas City, Missouri—the city from the dream—to be back working with the International House of Prayer and our church.

We should all desire to see more visions or have dreams from the Lord. I believe hunger is what truly creates response from heaven. In Daniel 7, Daniel is given an incredible vision and dream of things yet to come. What interests me about this chapter is how many times Daniel says "then I kept looking." It's like the Lord would reveal one part of the vision to him, but his curiosity and initiative is what unlocked the next part of the vision. Wouldn't it be truly amazing if everyone was walking around seeing visions from the Lord? It takes hunger, appetite for Him, and curiosity for the seer realm to be released!

Activation

I want to lead you into a closed vision with the Lord. To prepare for this, you might want to go somewhere quiet where there will be no interruptions.

First, how to do you relate to God? Do you relate to—and by *relate* I mean *talk to*—God the Father, Jesus, or Holy Spirit? Which form does God speak to you the most in this season of your life? Right now, for me it's Holy Spirit. Before we begin, I want to pray.

> *Lord, I just pray right now that Your presence would show up. Thank You that You are already here and resting on the person reading this. I pray that all distractions would be silenced right now in the blood of the Lamb. I just pray that You, Lord, would open our eyes to see and hear from You today. I bind the enemy from trying to come into this time or room and bring confusion. Thank You, Abba. Amen.*

Now, I want you to invite whoever you relate to the most right now into this vision. The Lord's going to show you a place first. What is in that place? What do you see? This might be a time to stop and take note of what you see. For me, I see right now a waterfall and a bird. Now take a moment to engage all your senses. Do you smell anything in this place? Can you taste anything in the air? What is the temperature like in this place? Try and engage your body as well. How do your feet feel? Are they resting in soft sand, or are they standing on hard ground? What about your arms? Do you feel water droplets on your arms or the warmth of the sun on them?

Now where is God in this vision? You might be surprised. He might approach you as Jesus or show up as a gentle dove. You might see the Lion of Judah approach you or see His presence in a whirlwind. What does He want to say to you or share with you? Now, does this seem contrary to Scriptures or seem to line up with His very nature? If you are the slightest bit unsure, take the time to stop here and pray, rebuking the enemy. Sometimes, the enemy will try and show up as a counterfeit in visions, and he needs to be rebuked. Now, go back to where you are in His presence.

Stay here until you feel like the vision is complete. Now ask the Lord to bring you back here next time and maybe show you more.

Thank You, Lord, for the way You gently guide us. Even though this might seem like new territory to some of us, I pray that You would show us more. God, I pray for the reader to experience open visions regularly. I pray that they would catch glimpses of Your presence showing up throughout their day. Open up our dream life to receive from You even in the night. Thank You, Lord, for what You showed and spoke to us today. I pray and seal everything up now in the blood of the Lamb. Amen.

Chapter 7

Choosing Faith or Fear

Some of us are just born with incredible faith to see the impossible. Most of us, though, are not naturally born with that level of faith. We long to be! We look at others' lives jealously; they seem to have incredible journeys because of the level of risk they take with God over and over again.

Maybe as children we have faith that unwaveringly will believe the unbelievable. I myself believed in Santa Claus until sixth grade, and also in my leprechaun friend who mysteriously had similar handwriting to my parents! As we grow up, though, our faith tends to dwindle off.

We may look at great heroes of the faith like Billy Graham, Kathryn Kuhlman, George Mueller, or Heidi Baker and think,

Wow! Why wasn't I given that measure of faith? God must have made a mistake when He created my weak, doubting little self! Granted, those people are truly heroes of the faith, but what we don't always see is the great amount of sacrifice they have made to attain that faith level.

Faith is developed out of great and extreme difficult situations. A trauma hits and *boom*—your faith level will hit you in the face right there. That is when we are all faced with the reality of what we truly believe, what we're going to listen to, and what we'll stand on.

One of my favorite faith stories in the Bible is the one about Shadrach, Meshach, and Abed-nego found in Daniel 3. How many of us can relate to being thrown into the fire at one point in our lives? Shadrach, Meshach, and Abed-nego are essentially set up for a cruel ending. They refuse to bow down to a golden image, and King Nebuchadnezzar becomes enraged with them. He gives them one last chance to bow down to his image, or he threatens to throw them into a fiery furnace and cook them alive. Their response is amazing!

> *If it be so, our God whom we serve is able to deliver us from the furnace of blazing fire; and He will deliver us out of your hand, O king. But even if He does not, let it be known to you, O king, that we are not going to serve your gods or worship the golden image that you have set up* (Daniel 3:17 NASB).

Even if God does not come through for them, they will still not waiver in their faith. This is a hard question I think many of us face. We want to believe that God is the God of the impossible, but then we all have those moments when we end up asking, *But God, where were You then?* Will we still choose to serve and believe in His faithfulness even when life doesn't work out according to how we planned?

Do we choose faith or fear in that moment?

In 2010 when we were in Mozambique with the Bakers, toward the end of our time there tragedy hit. I'll never forget that day. It was pouring rain, and my phone, which hardly ever worked, surprisingly rang, so I answered it. It was my aunt calling from the States—it was a miracle that she could even reach us. She broke the news to us. My father, a doctor who ran every day and was in perfect health, was in the emergency room of the hospital with blood clots found throughout his body. He apparently had a hidden gene unknown to us that caused him to be susceptible to blood clots. His leg was completely swollen with blood clots and artery damage, and his lungs also had clots in them. Things did not look so good.

So there we were. Do we choose faith or fear in that moment? Or a little bit of both! I remember having that horrible prayer, "Even if You take him, God, I will still love You." I found faith that I didn't even know I had. I remember days of hard conversations with family members back home as things got worse and worse, and I just had to keep declaring, "He will live!" Meanwhile, we were trying to find flights to get back home as quickly as possible.

We miraculously made it back home, and by that time my father was out of the hospital and at home with my mother and nurses caring for him. I have never seen my father that afraid in my life. The one person I knew to always be the steady rock in our family suddenly was a person awake at four in the morning, eyes bug-eyed with fear, talking like he'd had six shots of espresso. Fear gripped him. So Sam and I began to pray for his healing. We would share stories of miracles that we had been a part of in Africa to increase faith in the house. I walked through some hard doctor's appointments with my dad, when more fear was spoken into the situation.

A long story shortened—my dad did live! A combination of natural blood thinners (not the blood thinners the doctors wanted my dad to take) and prayer healed his body. He's now happily able to work out again and exercise with no problems. Blood clots are something he will probably always have to watch out for, but other than that his life is back to how it was before they discovered the gene.

That was years ago, but the story does swing back around. When I was six months pregnant, I had the thought, *Why not check for the gene? Maybe I carry it too.* I highly doubted it. Surely with all the flying I'd done to all these foreign countries and being in my 30s, doctors would have caught it by now and warned me if I had it. I was wrong! I remember the flood of emotion hitting me full on in the face as the doctor told me that test results came back positive, and that I am a carrier of the gene. Images flashed through my mind of my dad's leg swollen. Conversations I had had with my dad's doctors instantly came back to my mind, of him facing possibly the worst-case scenario of never having a fully functioning leg again.

And there we were again! Faith or fear? I had to meet with specialists who all encouraged me to start blood thinners instantly and continue them through my entire pregnancy. No matter how much I prayed, no matter how much research and outside input I received, I did not feel peace about going ahead with the injections. I am not encouraging people to go against the doctor's wisdom. I am encouraging people to do what they feel peace on and what they feel God has confirmed for them to do. In our case, it was to not take the injections. We also had already lost one child in a miscarriage, so suddenly I was considered a very high-risk case. However, there was an experience I had with the Lord, back before my dad's health issues, that had built my faith muscles and prepared me for these moments.

Fear or faith? Which one will you build

your life on? You will have to make

this choice over and over again.

Grand Canyon

Anyone who visits the Grand Canyon and takes in its beauty gains incredible respect for life. Standing on the cliff's edge there, time suddenly feels endless. The air seems still, and the quiet swallows you. Personally, I don't know how anyone can experience it without leaving wondering if there is a God. Its extraordinary sights are breathless. It is here, at the Grand Canyon, that I have had many encounters with God and angels.

Back when I first started having visions, I had never been to the Grand Canyon before. I remember being in a prayer meeting, and with my eyes closed suddenly I would be on the edge of the cliffs of the Grand Canyon. There Jesus would approach me Himself. The first time He took me there, that's all I saw. I just saw Jesus Himself smile at me, and I was undone. Just seeing that smile, my heart felt tickled with the joy and love of the Father.

One of my favorite visions at the Grand Canyon happened before I got married. I was back at the Grand Canyon, and I could see Jesus ahead of me standing at the edge of a cliff. I approached Him timidly because I had a sense that He was about to teach me a lesson that would be challenging. "Ana, what do you see?" He asked me as I approached Him.

"Well, Lord, I see the beautiful canyon and rock patterns created by the river that used to once be here. I see people down below trying to hike. I see a small cave across the way that looks like a tiny dot. It's beautiful up here!"

"Look closer," He said. "Quiet your mind first. What else do you see?"

I strained my eyes to try and see what He was focusing on. I couldn't see anything. So I closed my eyes and inwardly asked Holy Spirit to help me. Then I felt it. It wasn't something I could see at first but just sense. Just as when you can stand in a crowded area and then suddenly feel like someone is staring at you and you turn around and catch that person's eye, I felt something approaching me. Glancing down, I saw it. Way off in the distance, a small dot approached. As it got closer, I saw that it was a huge eagle—not a regular eagle that you would see out in the wild, but an eagle whose body from head to tail was at least eight feet long. Fear instantly pulsed through my body. I wasn't sure if I wanted to get too close to this huge creature, but it just kept coming closer and closer.

Finally, it was soaring back and forth just under the cliff. Jesus looked at me as if to answer my question of, *What am I supposed to do here?* "Jump off the ledge and onto that eagle," He told me.

Panic overwhelmed me. *What? No way! You know that I have a major fear of heights. Just me standing here on the cliff's edge with You is a miracle in itself,* I thought.

As if He could read my thoughts, He turned to me and smiled. "Ana. It's now that you have to choose. Fear or faith? Which one will you build your life on? You will have to make this choice over and over again, but I promise you, you can always trust Me. You may not understand them, but My ways are always best. Do you really trust me? Or do you trust yourself more? In your lifetime here on earth, I will call you to do things sometimes that you're not comfortable with or feel unprepared to do. In those moments, will you trust Me? Will you choose faith instead of fear? Today, you make your decision."

And with that, He was gone. I was left standing on the edge of this enormous cliff. Looking downward, my head started to buzz, and my heart felt like it was going to pound out of my chest. "But, God! It's so far! Couldn't we start this faith thing with like a five-foot drop instead of the Grand Canyon?" I cried out loud.

Then, His words rang in my head. "I will call you to do things sometimes that you're not always comfortable with."

The eagle just kept soaring underneath the ledge—back and forth, back and forth. It was like he was waiting for me. Back and forth he went, as I just kept looking on in terror. Images of my life just kept flashing through my head—people I had had my last conversations with. I truly thought that maybe this would be my end. Back and forth. Back and forth.

"OK, God. Here's the deal. I'm not some big shot faith healer! I'm just little, small Ana! Why would You want me to do this?" I yelled into the thin air. Back and forth. Back and forth the eagle soared.

Then a phrase popped into my head. "I am for you, not against you. I will be with you!"

Well, that's true, I thought. *I suppose it is better to do crazy things with God than be totally void of Him. I guess if I die, I get to see Him anyway!* I wasn't displaying the hugest amount of faith in this moment that I would be just fine.

So with that, I closed my eyes, yelled "I choose faith!" and jumped. Then, I fell! I fell and fell for what seemed like forever but was probably only a few seconds. Terror pulsed through my body, as all I could see was the whirling ground below. Then suddenly, I landed on something really hard. "Ouch!"

To my surprise, I was on the back of that giant eagle. Big and brown, from my viewpoint his body also resembled a giant cross. I was wrong about his size! What looked like eight feet in stature was actually more like twenty once I was actually riding on him. I gripped his feathers, holding on for dear life! We soared so quickly that I felt like my cheeks were being pushed into the back of my throat. Then the eagle did something surprising. It turned its head to look back at me and seemed to smile.

Did that eagle just smile at me? I wondered.

Then I heard His voice. "I told you I would be with you!" It was then that I realized I was riding on Holy Spirit.

Just like that, I was back in the prayer meeting. My body was covered with sweat. My clothes were soaked from the adrenaline. I looked at the time and at least an hour had passed.

One of my favorite biblical examples of someone who moved in incredible signs and wonders and had enormous faith in God is Moses. You know why I love him? He didn't start out with incredible faith. It's like we can follow his maturing in faith in Exodus. See, God had a mark on his life for great things even before he believed in himself. That encourages me immensely! We all know the story of Moses starting out as a Hebrew, hidden from Pharaoh's slaughter by floating down a river as a baby and being rescued by Pharaoh's own daughter, then growing up in the palace as Pharaoh's son. Follow the story in Exodus and eventually Moses meets his destiny with God. The presence of God shows up in the desert in a mighty way that rocks Moses' sandals off, and God asks him to do something that seems totally impossible to Moses. *"I will send you to Pharaoh, so that you may bring My people, the sons of Israel, out of Egypt"* (Exod. 3:10 NASB).

Now here's the part of the story I love. Moses' response! *"Who am I, that I should go to Pharaoh, and that I should bring the sons of Israel out of Egypt?"* (Exod. 3:11 NASB). Moses, who is known as one of the great heroes of faith, starts off a little shaky. I am so encouraged by this! Then God's response is just perfect, of course. He says, "Certainly I will be with you" (Exod. 3:12 NASB). My paraphrase: "Get your eyes off of yourself and set them on Me! I am the Living God who is capable of the impossible!"

I can't tell you how many times I am reminded of this by the Lord. Just when I allow fear to creep in the back door, God will take me back to that encounter with the eagle I had in the Grand Canyon, His voice ringing through my head, "Will you choose faith or fear?" Then He will lovingly nudge me by reminding me of Moses. If we only look toward ourselves and our own strength to accomplish something great, I think the majority of us would stop at that—just looking and never accomplishing anything at all. Our focus has to be cleared of our inward capabilities, fixated on Him. I think great heroes of the faith aren't automatically born with it.

> "Get your eyes off of yourself and set them on Me! I am the Living God who is capable of the impossible!"

I think it takes a daily choice of deciding to trust in Him. It's funny how although I chose to jump off that cliff in the Grand Canyon, Holy Spirit didn't catch me right away. He could have, but He didn't. Now every time I am faced with a hard decision where I have to choose to trust God beyond what I'm comfortable with, and maybe things don't work out right away how I would have wanted, I still have to choose to trust in Him. He will catch me!

I heard a message once preached by Bob Jones that I love to quote. He said something like, "There is something greater than faith, and that is trust. There is something greater than trust, and that is rest. It's not just about going across Niagara Falls in a wheelbarrow eating peanuts. It's about taking a nap while in that wheelbarrow!"

Activation Prayer

God, right now I pray for more faith. I confess my own lack of faith sometimes—a lot of times! Especially when things are hard. God, I trust you with my health, with my finances, with my future, with my dreams, with my family and friends, and with my safety. I choose faith today and command fear to leave. I will not partner with fear any longer but partner with the Living God who is capable of the impossible. You have great things for me! You have not left me, and never will! You see great potential in me. Along with choosing faith, I let go of fear, which has become my safety net. Choosing fear seems safer at times, but the safest place I can be is in Your arms, in Your will for my life. I break my agreement right now with fear in the name of Jesus. I will do as the worship song says and "climb this mountain with my hands wide open. I lean not on my own understanding. My life is in the hands of the Maker of heaven." Amen.

What's God asking you to do right now? Something He's asking will demand faith. Holy Spirit, come. Take a moment here and pause and ask the Lord to show you a picture or speak to you.

Thank You, Father. Now God, I pray that You would show us what might be standing in the way of us accomplishing this. (Take a moment and pause here and ask Holy Spirit to show you if there is anything hindering or blocking you to stand in faith with this.) God, give us wisdom if there is anything You are asking us to do to remove this hindrance.

I pray for an increase and impartation of faith to fall right now. Thank You, God, for the great things You are going to accomplish with our lives! Amen.

Discussion Questions

1. What's your cliff that will take a leap of faith?

2. What image comes to mind when you think of Holy Spirit?

Chapter 8

Three Other Rooms in Heaven

I'm no expert on heaven. I've heard and read the testimonies from different people who have all claimed to have been there, and they all sound amazing. All I can do is just write and share from a firsthand perspective the different rooms the Lord has taken me to in heaven.

Mailer Room

It's one of the busiest places to visit! It's one of the craziest rooms and also the most intriguing places I've ever been to. I call this room "the giant mailer room."

I think previously, before I had ever experienced heaven, I would have thought that all the rooms in heaven are super peaceful. You know, like with fat angel babies floating on clouds, strumming their instruments. Although I'm sure there are some fat babies in heaven, now I know that my expectation of what heaven would be like was so far from how glorious and magnificent it really is.

One day, I had been praying and asking the Lord to show me new places in heaven, and He took me to a new room. We walked first, hand in hand down a large hallway—that glorious hallway I've learned to love. The place felt warm. Not just a warm temperature measured in Celsius or Fahrenheit, but an internal warmth and joy filled me. Like a kid waiting at the top of the stairs Christmas morning in anticipation for everyone to wake up as he sees all the presents waiting for him under the tree—that's how I felt as I walked hand in hand with my Savior down this hallway.

There were many huge doors I saw, and I'm sure there are many more that I didn't see—the hallway seemed to have no end. Then we came to a door and Jesus stopped me in front of it. In all my times traveling with the Lord in heaven and going to different rooms with Him, He always does the same thing. He will show me a door that leads to a room in which He wants to teach me something, but He will always stop and give me the choice to open the door. There have been times when I just dive right in and it seems I cannot get the door open quick enough; then there are other times when I feel a hesitation—like maybe what's behind that door might be hard for me to face or require something of me that will cause my faith to be stretched!

This time, though, I opened the door with excitement and eagerness to see what was inside. To my surprise, I was suddenly caught up in a whoosh of Holy Spirit activity. We entered the room and entered what looked like chaos, but it was beautiful, organized chaos! Angels bustled back and forth, to and fro, going to shelves and carrying different parcels in their arms. The parcels were of all different sizes and colors. The angels would go to the giant shelves and search for a specific package. Once they found it, they would then drop down to the earth below with the package in arm like they were on a mission. I could see them drop down because the room had no floor, nor could I see the ceiling.

Never give up partnering with Me and asking!

I just stood mesmerized, watching the angels busily work. "What are they doing?" I asked the Lord.

"Well, they are taking answers to the prayers of saints down below. Each one is specifically assigned for the delivery of these special packages."

Then I looked around more. I noticed something peculiar. There were some angels frantically moving quickly to deliver, but there were others who were just standing by the shelf not moving.

"Why are those ones not delivering the packages?" I asked the Lord.

"They are waiting," He smiled back at me.

I looked back at Him puzzled. I clearly did not understand what was going on here.

"They are waiting for my saints down below to pray and ask for what it is they need. For you see, these are the answer to their prayers, yet some are afraid to ask. Ask, and it will be given to you; knock, and it will be opened (see Matt. 7:7). Some of these packages are timely too. The angels are waiting for my permission to carry out their mission. My timing is always good and always perfect, for I am the Author and Creator of the universe. But Ana, you must always ask. Never give up partnering with Me and asking! I want you to look up and forever remember this sight."

I looked up. As far as my eyes could see, these shelves reached up and up into the heavens, and thousands and thousands of parcels were waiting and lining the shelves. There the most beautiful angels just stood waiting, looking toward Jesus for direction, never taking their eyes off Him.

Spending time with Jesus in this room has forever marked me. I used to think, *Do my prayers really matter to God? Does He really hear them?* Now the scripture has meaning: *"Be anxious for nothing, but in everything by prayer and supplication with thanksgiving let your requests be made known to God"* (Phil. 4:6 NASB). I remember that mailer room and the shelves upon shelves of answers just waiting to be released. Our God is a God who cares for His children.

Worship Leader

Then another time, I was taken up in the Spirit to heaven. It was prophesied over my life that I would be able to see up Jacob's ladder and see the angels of heaven (see Gen. 28:12). Some of my visions with God have been like that. I will see a giant, fiery, golden ladder fall down from the sky or ceiling, if I am inside a building at the time. On it I will see angels moving up and down. There is always an invitation for me to go up the ladder if I want. I use to be afraid of going up, but now I beg God for more ladder experiences.

The Lord was orchestrating the release of His presence in response to the worship of His saints.

So this vision started with a stairway from heaven coming down. At the time, I was in my room just listening to some worship music. I saw the ladder and saw an angel motion for me to come up with him. So I went. Once I reached what seemed like the top of the ladder, I found myself in that giant hallway again. This time one of the doors was highlighted. It seemed to have a glow coming from behind the door because I could see light streaming in the hallway from the cracks around the door.

I opened the door with excitement. What I saw amazed me! There was a room with no floor or ceiling. The room seemed to travel up forever. At first my eyes had to adjust because the multi-colored lights streaming from the center of that room were too much for my eyes to handle at first.

Then I saw Him. My eyes fixed on the center of the room, on the one I love. Jesus was there with His back turned to me. I could see Him frantically but beautifully waving his arms around. It looked really odd at first. *Lord, what are you doing?* I thought. Then, as if God had heard my question, my spiritual ears were opened to hear the sounds of the room.

It was glorious! I could hear the most beautiful worship and music that I have ever heard in my lifetime. I could hear what seemed like millions and millions of people singing. And there was my Lord, orchestrating with His arms the beams of light.

What are you doing with the light? I raised a question again.

Just then He turned around and looked at me smiling. "Come and see!"

I was kind of hesitant then to approach Him because there was no floor to the room, and I am used to gravity. I seriously thought that I was going to just drop through the room and fall out of heaven! Then I heard the word "Trust" in my head, so I decided to just run toward Him.

That is where I saw what the King was seeing. Looking down below our feet, I could see the earth! It seemed so small compared to where we were.

"Look closer," Jesus implored me.

So I did. I saw different parts of the earth being highlighted. Many different parts were giving off a light at different times. As they would illuminate, the Lord would wave His arms and I could then see the light beams of heaven being released down from the room to those very locations. It was incredible! The Lord was orchestrating the release of His presence in response to the worship of His saints.

Strategy Room

There is one room that the Father has taken me to several times at different periods of my life. Usually it is in a time of great transition or shift. I call this the "strategy room." It is a room like no other. Always when I approach this door, I feel a little hesitancy in my spirit and anticipation for what the Lord is going to show me.

One time I went here in a vision. Jesus was there waiting for me at the entrance to a giant, oak-looking door. As my hand reached for the door knob, I suddenly had the revelation that waiting on the other side of that door was a lot of commotion.

I turned the knob and the door threw itself open. There I saw angels like I had never seen before. Up until this point in my walk with seeing in the spiritual realm, I had never seen angels that looked so large, scary, and warrior-like. Jesus led me in and showed me around the room. I saw angels dressed in all sorts of different armor. They all looked huge and fiercely intimidating. There was one exceptionally large one I could see standing in the center of the room. It looked as if he was chief commander, showing the other angels where to go and what to do. That is, of course, until Jesus walked in the room, and all the angels stopped to take commands from Him.

Jesus asked for something from the chief commanding angel of operations, and that angel returned carrying a large rolled-up scroll. The paper looked worn but yet had gold lacing the edges. Jesus then motioned for me to follow Him.

Intimidated, I followed closely behind Him, trying to not make eye contact with any of the warrior angels. There was a large, oak-looking table on one side of the room. Jesus led me to it and then spread out the scroll. The scroll unraveled and covered the entire table.

Intrigued, I first looked at Jesus, questioning in my head, *Am I allowed to look at this?*

"It's OK. Come take a look," Jesus responded out loud.

I peered over the table and looked at the paper. At first I saw…nothing. Literally, nothing! Then I remembered to pray. So I closed my eyes and in my head said, *Lord, please open my spiritual eyes.*

When I opened my eyes, there before me I saw the paper come alive. Images were moving and it took me a while to be able to decipher what they were. Then one set of images really grabbed my attention. I saw a glimpse of myself except I looked a little different than I currently looked. The next image I saw was a picture of a man with me. Then following was a picture of the two of us in Africa with Heidi and Rolland Baker. Following that picture was a moving picture of a plane taking off. Following that was a picture of us holding a child. Lastly after that, I saw a picture of another plane taking off.

That was it. The vision was over. At the time, I just wrote it all down and said, "Um…thanks God." Now I know why He showed all those images to me. Years later I was struggling with wanting to go to Africa to work with the Bakers, but I knew the timing just wasn't right. It was then, in that moment, that I remembered this specific vision I had from the strategy room. I remembered that it wasn't until I was married that I would be going to Africa. I am 100 percent sure now, after having been to Africa, that this was wisdom from the Lord. Now that my husband and I have a child, I'm wondering where that next image of us going off in a plane will lead.

A few other times I've been allowed back to this room. I call this room the "strategy room" because I am always taken to the large table where a scroll is laid out, and I am shown heaven's blueprints.

Conclusion

God's such a complex personhood to understand. The Trinity is one of the most complex yet beautiful relationships I have ever known. Every time the Lord takes me to heaven, I feel like I am getting the privilege to know more of His nature—the authority that He carries, the way He always gives me a choice to pursue Him and yet He will always pursue me, the way He answers my prayers and shares life with me, the wild worshiper and creator He is! There are just too many facets of the One we love to be grasped, but I love the ways He slowly shows Himself to me in a new glimpse. Hopefully you have been shown something new about His character and nature also by reading about heaven.

Activation Prayer

Lord God, first I thank You for the gift of heaven. Thank You that You have saved us all from a lifetime of suffering and that one day we will have the choice to come dwell with You in eternal glory! Father, right now I just pray for every person reading this book, that You will open their spiritual eyes to see a glimpse of Your glory. Lord, I pray that You would open a facet of heaven to them. Encounter them, Lord, not so that they could have an awesome experience from You and get a rush out of it, but encounter them so that they could know You are near and pursing them. Encounter us all so we can fall more in love with You. Amen.

Discussion Questions

1. Which of the three rooms is most intriguing to you and why?

2. In that room, go back and look at my interaction with Jesus. What does it show about His nature?

Chapter 9

Healing with the Seer Anointing

God's creativity never ceases to amaze me! Looking at the life of Jesus, we can see many different ways Jesus healed the sick. So I pose the question—if there was a set formula, A+B+C=healing, would we keep pressing in to the Father for healing? In all the different ways I have seen God move and heal people, every time I have learned to lean into Holy Spirit and ask Holy Spirit how He wants to heal today, and almost every time proves to be different.

Biblically speaking, Jesus heals people differently each time. From the healing of a blind man by spitting on the ground and smearing clay over his eyes (see John 9:6), to touching a coffin and bringing the dead back to life (see Luke 7:14), to healing a man's withered hand by commanding him to stretch it out (see Mark 3:5), God displays His creativity. By examining the Scriptures, you can discover even more examples of the creativity of God in the way He heals people.

If there was a set formula, A + B + C = healing, would we keep pressing in to the Father for healing?

Unto His Glory: Testimonies

There we were in South Africa, visiting family, fresh out of leaving the mission field of the "bush-bush" of Mozambique. (Technically, we ended up stranded there because of flight complications and had the privilege to stay with my husband's family for a short respite.) On Sunday, we all gathered up to go to a friend's church. What a shocker it was going from the bush-bush church of Mozambique, where there are no chairs but dirt floors and no air conditioning, to this church with pews and projector screens. Halfway through the message, I leaned into my husband and said, "Sam, I really feel like there is someone here who needs healing prayer that we are supposed to pray for. What should we do? I don't know if they even believe in healing prayer here."

He immediately responded to me, "I just had the same feeling! I don't know. Let's just wait until the end of the service and see what God says to do."

So we waited. At the very end the minister said, "And if anyone needs healing prayer, come on forward and we have teams of people who would love to bless you with prayer."

And there he was. We watched a guy painfully and slowly walk from the back of the church all the way up to the front. It took a lady helping him walk for him to make it up there. "That's him," I said to my husband.

"Yep," he agreed. So we approached him and the team that was praying over him and asked if we could join.

To make a long story short, the rest of the team took off, and we were left with just the man and his friend who helped him walk up to the front. It turns out that he had nerve damage all the way throughout his entire body and was in constant excruciating pain. So we began to pray. My hands started to feel warm to touch, so I placed them on his back and began to pray. "Oooooo," he suddenly said. "Something feels different. I feel a tingling happening."

"Tingling is good," we responded excitedly.

We continued to pray. Honestly though, tingling was the only change happening for this gentleman, and we didn't want to just leave him like that. So as we continued to pray, I felt Holy Spirit urge me to start singing over him. So I did! I started to just sing a worship song over him as my husband continued to pray. Together we ushered this guy into the presence of the Lord. By worshiping, the presence of the Lord fell in the room thick. Even this guy, who had never experienced a presence like this, responded, "You guys...you guys carry something. You really do walk with God!"

"Yes, we love Him. Now how's your neck? Test it out," I responded. He began to move his neck and slowly but gradually it loosened up. Then we continued to worship together and have him keep testing out his back, knees, arms, and toes. Eventually, that man walked out of that chapel completely healed proclaiming the name of Jesus! It turns out it was his birthday that day. God is so good!

This is a wonderful example of gradual healing. Just like in Mark 8:22-26 where Jesus heals a blind man but He heals gradually instead of instantaneously, so was the gentleman's healing that day in South Africa. Why didn't Jesus just heal that blind man right away? He could. He is God, after all. Maybe it is to encourage us believers to keep pressing in for healing even when we are not seeing instant results.

Another time, my husband and I were walking with our ministry team trekking through the foothills of the Himalayas. As we came up a path close to a local village, suddenly a tiny crowd of eyes started popping up over the mountainside. As you can imagine, a group of Caucasian foreigners drew the interest of the local village. Right then I heard Holy Spirit say "stomachs." This is an example of how to use the gift of the word of knowledge that is talked about in the Bible. That's all I heard! Nothing more than that—just "stomachs." So through our translators I asked the crowd if anyone had stomach problems and needed healing. Almost every person raised their hands! Our team immediately started praying for them and people were completely healed that day. Then we invited them to come and bring their entire village to our event that night where we would be showing the Jesus film and preaching. Many people came to know the Lord through this event. It started with just a simple word from Holy Spirit. It was a snowball effect. By taking that simple word from Holy Spirit, "stomachs," and getting over my own fear to ask, people got touched, were ministered to, and then later brought the rest of their village to meet the foreigners and hear about Jesus. We never know what the outcome will be to our simple response to the Holy Spirit.

Using the gift of seeing in the Spirit also helps tremendously when doing healing ministry. I used to be on the healing teams of Bethel Church in Redding, California. Conference mode for the healing rooms is a crazy time! Hundreds upon hundreds of people from all over the world come through the healing rooms in just a short amount of time. It's exhilarating and exciting to watch what Jesus does around the room. During conferences, we moved the healing rooms into the large auditorium where church is usually held. There, you can just scan around the room and watch God's presence touching people in different ways. You can feel excitement and expectation in the air. People in one corner that day were dancing; in another part of the room I could hear people laughing hysterically as God touched them with joy. I was running around the back of the room with one lady as God completely healed her ankle and we felt like running for joy! If you close your eyes and just listen, you can hear Jesus touching people all throughout the room. It's glorious!

So there I was, put on a ministry team. As we were looking around the room, asking the Lord who to pray for next, a *giant* angel caught my attention. He was *huge!* I am not the best at guessing height or distances, but I would say this angel was at least 20 feet tall. He looked amazing! His clothes seemed to be on fire, and a blinding light was coming from behind him—so much that it was hard to even keep watching him. I did make out, though, that he was carrying a spine. (My dad's a chiropractor, so I grew up used to seeing spinal cords, and I think I even owned a spine keychain at one point!) The angel saw me, looked at me, winked, and smiled. *Hm*, I thought. *What's he up to?* I told my team, "Um…I think we should go follow that angel!" So we did! We followed him to a lady who was sitting in a wheelchair. I witnessed the angel put the new spine in her back, and then he was gone.

What is interesting is that this lady didn't feel healed right then. My team and I told her, "We just saw an angel put a new spine in your back. I think God's healing you! You should test it out." She looked at us pretty skeptically. So we gently held her hands, and asked her to try standing up. She did! Then we asked her to try stretching from side to side. She did, reluctantly. Years of chronic pain had left this lady pretty doubtful and hopeless that God could just touch her just like that, without anyone even praying over her. Eventually, through us telling her what we had seen and convincing her to test it out, her faith grew and she began to believe that God truly had touched her. As her faith grew, so did the increase of healing being released over her body, and eventually this lady left that day without needing her wheelchair anymore. *"Daughter, your faith has made you well; go in peace and be healed of your affliction"* (Mark 5:34 NASB).

There is another type of healing that is amazing to watch the power of God work through. Whole books have been written on inner healing and its incredible effects on freeing our body, soul, and mind. I have witnessed firsthand the effects of the power of God moving through someone as they are walked through breaking off lies and agreements they have made with the enemy.

When my husband and I were in India with Iris Ministries, we had the privilege of getting to work with a Youth with a Mission base. Friends of ours are the leaders, so they asked us to come and speak on the healing power of God to a team that was visiting and also to their base staff. After we gave a short talk on the healing, we broke up and began praying over the staff. That day many people received healing, but one particular story stays locked in my memory.

As I laid hands on one of the visiting staff, I immediately heard the words "inner healing, deep-rooted lies." So I began to just pray in tongues and ask Holy Spirit to either show me what some of those lies were or to show the lady I was ministering to. Soon after, I began hearing lies. "She believes she's not valuable; she believes she has no voice; she suffers from night terrors." So instead of just saying, "Hey, so you have this…" I asked her, "I was just wondering, do you suffer from nightmares ever?" This broke the lock that seemed to be keeping her in isolation. Fear of vulnerability had locked her into suffering, pain, and insecurity for years, but through Holy Spirit's help we were able to pull out some of those lies and break off wrong agreements that day. It was beautiful to witness the whole team, coming around her as she walked toward her healing of old wounds and lies, and giving her the support and love she was truly needing. The church body has to be careful that we do not ever shame people with their pain. It's important when walking someone through inner healing to step back and think, *Hey, if I was in their shoes right now dealing with all this, how would I want to be treated?*

Healing Cross

Let's go back to the cross! Without the power of the death and resurrection of the One we love, our prayers for healing would be useless. When our King cried out "*It is finished!*" it is in this we can place our hope (John 19:30). If our hope is in man or our own capabilities, then we have lost sight of the cross and are lining ourselves up for failure and disappointment.

Healing the sick equals staying in touch and intimate with the Father.

Never do I go into ministry thinking that I know how to do everything. Don't misunderstand what I am saying here. Through Christ I can do everything. The Word says in Mark 11:23 and Philippians 4:13 that if I have no doubt in my heart and my faith is in Him I can do all things. I believe this is where many people moving in healing ministry often slip up and stumble. Once their ministry gains some momentum and perhaps recognition, they slip up and start believing in their own capabilities rather than their utmost dependence on Him. Without intimacy with the One who is worthy of all our adoration and love, our sinful nature has a way of taking over. There are many people with a strong anointing who have never been able to rise to the calling on their lives and fall short of all that God called them to do for this exact reason. Intimacy with Him and dependence on Him is everything. That's probably why God's first commandment is to "*love the Lord your God with all your heart, and with all you soul, and with all your mind*" (Matt. 22:37 NASB).

So what can we learn about healing the sick? There's a formula that always worked for our greatest example, Jesus. Healing the sick equals staying in touch and intimate with the Father. Whenever I lay hands on people to pray for them, I always first ask the Father what He wants to do in that moment. There have been numerous times when a person came up to me asking for healing prayer for a specific part of their body and I heard the Father say something different. I usually then just say, "I know you've asked for prayer for _____, and I'm going to pray for that too, but here's what I hear the Lord saying _____. Does that mean anything to you?" That usually unlocks something much deeper that the Lord wants to heal first, and then the other healing comes next.

I love partnering with what the Lord wants to do when His healing presence shows up.

Activation Prayer

God, I pray that You would make our ears ever so sensitive to hear from the Spirit what You are up to when we pray for people. God, help us to move with the compassion of the Father first as we lay hands on and pray to heal the sick. Your Word says "It is finished" on the cross, so we claim this now over ourselves and over the people we will pray for.

Lord, I pray right now that You would train us to hear Your voice with clarity. I pray the gift of words of knowledge and prophecy would fall on the readers right now. I pray that You would open our spiritual eyes to see what You are doing in the room during ministry times. Amen.

Practicalities

Practically, now, there are a few things that I think might help encourage your gift of healing. We are all called to heal the sick. In Matthew 10:8 Jesus commands His disciples to go out and "*heal the sick.... Freely you received, freely give*" (NASB).

As a way to practice hearing the voice of God with clarity while praying for people, start paying attention to the little ideas or thoughts that may randomly come into your mind as you lay hands on them. Then find a simple yet humble way to phrase what you're sensing, such as, "I'm learning to hear from God. I just keep sensing this _____," or, "The phrase _____ keeps coming into my mind, and I'm wondering if that means anything to you?" You are stepping out in faith, but still maintaining a teachable spirit.

Close your eyes if it helps. When I first started praying for people, I would get so distracted by seeing what was happening in the physical realm that I would struggle to see in the spiritual realm or even hear from God clearly. Staying connected with the Father and dependent on Him unlocks His very nature. There is no sickness in heaven! His desire is for everyone to walk in freedom and wholeness.

Discussion Questions

1. When praying for people, how do you hear from God? Is it primarily through seeing, hearing, or sensing?

2. What way of hearing from God do you wish to grow in?

Chapter 10

Facing the Spirit of Death

There are many different seasons the Lord carries us through as believers. There is a time to rest, a time to run, a time to press and persevere, a time to fast, etc. I believe there is also a time to *stand* and make war on the enemy! Scripture says, "No weapon that is formed against you will prosper" (Isa. 54:17 NASB). Yes, God fights our victories, but He also equips us to partner with Him and make *war* on the enemy.

> *For our struggle is not against flesh and blood, but against the rulers, against the powers, against the world forces of this darkness, against the spiritual forces of wickedness in the heavenly places. Therefore, take up the full armor of God, so that you will be able to resist in*

the evil day, and having done everything, to **stand firm**
(Ephesians 6:12-13 NASB).

If there is anything I have learned the most from being overseas as a missionary in some really dark places, it is how to worship Jesus despite the darkness and make war on the enemy. There are many testimonies I could share here about warring against the enemy, but specifically I want to share about the time he almost took life from me.

I was on a ministry trip with a team from the International House of Prayer to New Orleans for Mardi Gras. As a seer, walking down Bourbon Street during Mardi Gras was a pretty intense experience. Demonic worship, sexual perversion, alcoholism, jealousy—the list could go on of what spirits are present during Mardi Gras. Just before we left for New Orleans, I found out I was pregnant. Like every mother's natural instinct, I immediately felt a little fear about my protection while doing ministry on those crowded, crazy streets without my husband with me. I prayed about it and heard the Lord say, "I will be with you," so I went anyway.

Once we got there, the ministry time on the streets wasn't actually where I came up against the most attack from the enemy. Through a line of connections I ended up getting to work with a young church girl who actually had attempted suicide a couple of times right before our team arrived. We met together a few times, and I was able to counsel her through some deep wounds. She wasn't open to receiving prayer, so I was only able to counsel her.

One specific time when the enemy came at me strong was when I first met her. I had just come back to the church to rest after ministering on the streets with my team for a couple of hours. When I walked in through the doors of the church, I saw it immediately. The spirit of death was looming around the corner in the chapel. *Eeekk!* It was hideous! I don't know how I knew it was the spirit of death; I just instantly did. I feel like Holy Spirit just told me in that moment, so I knew what I was up against. I looked around the chapel, and there was one of the teams just getting back from being out doing ministry, talking and laughing together, totally oblivious to what was in the room. And then I spotted her. There, all folded up into one of the couches sleeping, was a young girl who looked about fifteen. I could see that the spirit of death had his eyes fixated on her, but then he would also scarily glance at me.

"You have no authority to be here tormenting me! I am covered in the blood of the Lamb! You have no authority against the power of my God!"

Not knowing what to do at the moment, I just walked as quietly as I could (as if that would make a difference!) past the demonic spirit and went in my room to lie down. I felt exhausted and just wanted to rest. After only five minutes of shutting my eyes, I woke up feeling complete panic. A cold wind had whisked through the room, and suddenly the room felt dark, cold, and scary. I felt terror shoot through my body, causing my heart to pound quickly. There he was in the corner. The spirit of death had followed me back to my place of rest.

Instantly, I began hemorrhaging and started getting contractions! I had already lost my first baby, and these symptoms were all too familiar to me. Fear and pain surged through my body.

The spirit of death looked at me furiously.

Pain increased, and hemorrhaging continued.

He moved closer to me.

"No, God," I shouted out, wincing in pain. "You promised me this baby would live! Where are You?"

It moved closer to me. Fear pulsated through my body. I could hardly breathe. Fear and pain were taking over.

Then suddenly, I felt angry. I went from total fear to complete rage at this spirit of death. These literally were the words out of my mouth toward that demonic spirit: "How dare you!" I shouted out. "You have no authority to be here tormenting me! I am covered in the blood of the Lamb! You have no authority against the power of my God!"

The spirit of death took one step back at that point. The pain eased up a bit. And then he laughed. One of the most scary, disgusting sounds I have ever heard came out of his mouth. His eyes shot back at me, glowing red like blood.

"You can't do anything! Your baby will die! Where's your God now!" he responded back.

He took a much larger step toward me, and pain shot deep down into my abdomen. Contractions and hemorrhaging began to increase. The pain literally knocked me to my knees. Crumbled over on the ground, I began to pray in tongues.

"Worship Me," I heard God say. "Remember the promises."

In that moment my worship wasn't this booming voice. No, no! I pitifully started singing worship songs in pain.

"How great is my God! Sing with me how great is my God, and you shall see how great, how great are You God!"

The demonic power started shrieking and shrinking. He backed away, and then I could stand up again.

Whoa! What a shift happened in my spirit when I saw the power that my little worship had against the spirit of death! Then suddenly my voice became awesome! Or at least I like to think so. I started belting out at the top of my lungs, "Death you have no hold on me! God you have the victory! Death you have no hold on me! God you have the victory!"

I probably sang that over and over for ten minutes, and something happened. The atmosphere changed. No longer did I feel fear. I was in pain and still hemorrhaging, but seeing that spirit of death loose his power gave me courage to war!

Then I began to declare, "I declare right now that you have no authority here. God has promised me that this baby will live! I have seen this baby already, and I know that it is a warrior in the spirit like its momma! You are messing with the wrong family right now!" The spirit of death began to shrink. He now looked smaller than me—and I'm only 5 feet 4 inches.

"This baby will live a life where it walks in tremendous faith. This baby is mighty and carries an anointing of joy! It shall live in the name of the Lord. I will teach this baby to see in the spirit, and it will wreak havoc on you and all your friends!" Shrinking more, the demon moved as far away from me as he could into the corner of the room.

"Oh, get ready, because this is a child who is protected by God and will be a tremendous warrior for the Kingdom! And you, you must leave *now!* This battles is done, and God has won! Get out now in the name of Jesus!"

A prophet in Africa had given me a sword in the spirit to use in battlefields, and I waved my sword at him now. With that, the spirit of death shrieked and left the room.

Right then, the hemorrhaging and contractions completely stopped! Exhausted, I crashed into my bed for a nap. When I woke up a couple of hours later and I pulled back the covers, my body was entirely covered in angelic feathers!

The atmosphere changed. No longer did I feel fear. I was in pain and still hemorrhaging, but seeing that spirit of death loose his power gave me courage to war!

I went and took a pregnancy test right then, just to make sure after all that hemorrhaging that I was still pregnant. Sure enough, I was! After that day, the rest of my pregnancy was supernatural, and I now have a beautiful, healthy baby girl—Veera. She is currently only six months old, but I know she can see in the spirit already. One day an angel walked in the room when I was nursing her. Veera stopped eating, looked at the angel, and then began chatting and laughing with it.

Making War: Application

What's your posture in the spirit? When the enemy comes at you and tries to wreak havoc on your life, what do you want your position to look like? Have discouragement and disappointment become the crutches you fall back on? What about fear? It's so hard not to sink into fear when the enemy strikes hard. I write from personal experience. Trust me! My husband and I have had many encounters with the enemy's attacks. The more we step out in ministry and faith, the more he comes to discourage us.

But God is bigger. Simple as that! Let's get back to the simplicity of the gospel. The devil wants to be like God, but he is not. So many times, especially when we are under attack, our focus can be fixated on the power of the enemy. Spiritual warfare is real! The enemy's attacks are real and strong at times. I do believe, though, that the more our focus lies on his power to strike us down, the more power and authority he is given to be there. Our God is powerful. With a word He spoke Creation into being. When a horrible storm came to destroy the disciples of Jesus, *"He got up and rebuked the winds and the sea, and it became perfectly calm"* (Matt. 8:26 NASB).

The next time you find yourself in a battlefield with the enemy, shift your focus! When I battled the spirit of death for my daughter's life, one thing I did not do but I know helps in overcoming the enemy is reading Scripture or saying scriptures from memory. *"For the word of God is living and active and sharper than any two-edged sword"* (Heb. 4:12 NASB).

The enemy's battle plan is always to come *"steal and kill and destroy"* (John 10:10). So remember the promises the Lord has spoken over you! It's always the enemy's tactic to discourage us from fulfilling our destinies and the plans God has for our future. When I felt most afraid and at my lowest point battling the spirit of death, the Lord reminded me, "Remember the promises." I feel like that's when my focus shifted. I shifted from only seeing the pain and fear, or the enemy's power, to, *Oh, but here's what my God says!* This encouraged my faith.

> ## The power of our worship, faith in Him, and declaration looses the power of darkness off of our lives.

Faith is the strongest weapon we have against the enemy. Scriptures reveal that many times Christ says, "Go, your faith has healed you," or a different way of looking at it, "Go, your faith has caused the enemy to lose his grip over you." The enemy comes to steal your faith that God is who He says He is and that He will do what He says he will do. So in times of war, declare it! The power of our worship, faith in Him, and declaration looses the power of darkness off of our lives.

> *And let us run with endurance the race that is set before us, **fixing our eyes on Jesus,** the author and perfecter of faith, who for the joy set before Him endured the cross, despising the shame, and has sat down at the right hand of the throne of God (Hebrews 12:1-2).*

Discussion Questions

1. When spiritual warfare is strong, how can you war against the enemy differently than you've been doing?

2. Of the different ways I warred with the spirit of death, what struck you the most?

Chapter 11

The Glorious Cross

Recently, as a new mom one day I found myself struggling to keep my peace and joy. It had been an extremely difficult day with my daughter. She was in a pattern of only going down for two 45-minute naps, which was allowing me no personal time to get refreshed or get anything done!

I put her down, and then I found myself frantically grabbing my Bible for a moment of refreshment with the Father. Flipping open to the Psalms, I began speed reading, trying to ingest as much of the Scriptures as I could because I knew my time was limited.

Putting down my Bible, realizing this wasn't refreshing me at all, I cried out to the Father in desperation. "Lord, would

You just take me up to heaven? It's been a while since I've been there, and I need to be refreshed by You!"

Bam! Just like that, I found myself no longer sitting folded up in the corner of my living room couch but suddenly walking through a ginormous hallway in heaven with the Lord.

Hand in hand we walked down the hallway that seemed to go on forever. The air felt warm; there was an expression of love in the air. We walked past wooden door after wooden door.

"Lord, would You just take me up to heaven?"

Suddenly, we stopped in front of a door. This door was unlike any other door I had seen before in heaven. It was a worn looking door, it's wood deteriorating and peeling off. An old brass knob hug on it, looking like it was barely hanging on. At first I thought, *If I touch it, the knob will surely fall off.* Holes in the creases around the edge of the door revealed light from the other side. The appearance of this door proved its well-use.

Something always happens when I approach doors in heaven that Jesus has led me to. The first is that as I approach the door I can often feel what is on the other side. Sometimes I have to just look with my spiritual eyes through the door, to see what's on the other side. There have been rooms I have been led to where the presence of the King is so strong that I cannot enter, so I just get a glance from the outside of the room. Often, I can feel the emotion of what's on the other side of that door—peace, excitement, joy, laughter, etc. Second, I always wonder if Jesus will go with me into that room. Sometimes He does; sometimes He doesn't.

This time when I approached the door, I felt fear. I don't know how to explain it other than that. I know that there is no fear in heaven, but I truly felt afraid. I could feel that whatever the Lord was allowing me to see on the other side of the door was going to be intense. The closer I got to the door, the intensity weighed heavier and heavier.

Finally, I approached the knob. I looked at the Lord and thought, *Aren't You going to go in there with me?* He shook His head—no.

I reached out and grabbed for the doorknob, and immediately I felt a powerful rush hit my entire body. The presence of God was so thick, so strong, that I barely hung on. But I hung on! I hung on, because it's all I knew to do. I truly felt the fear of the Lord in such a strong way that it felt like the wind had been knocked out of me. My body went limp, but I still clung to that brass doorknob with all my strength.

It was then that I was allowed to see through the door to what was on the other side. I don't understand why I saw what I did in heaven, but there He was. I saw the cross. It was glorious—horrific and glorious! My King, the one I love, hung on that cross. The cross dripped with blood. It was gruesome and yet beautiful. The power of God was so strong.

"Lord, I want to go in there!" through my tears I cried out to God. I wanted to be as close to Him as I could.

The Father shook his head, *No.*

No matter how much I tried to turn the knob I couldn't. My own strength was nothing compared to the tangible power of God coming through that door, through that old doorknob. Wave after wave of power and love hit me. It pulsated through my body, causing me to shrink lower and lower to the ground until I was on my knees, just reaching up, hanging on to His presence through that doorknob.

His love was too much! It was more than I had ever felt in my life. The reality of the cross had me undone. I was wrecked by His love and presence. Sweat dripped from my body as it took all my strength to hang on.

Then, He looked at me. Tears filled the creases of his eyes.

Why can't I go in there, God? I mean, I'm a Christian! I'm in love with You, and You love me. I know Your forgiveness that took place on the cross. I know Your love! I thought.

Hearing my thoughts and looking at me through those pools in His eyes, He replied, "Ana, you don't know My love!"

The weight of it hit me like bricks on my chest. It still does!

"What! I don't know Your love? Of course I do!" This felt like Christianity 101.

"You don't know," was His response.

With that, I melted. I couldn't hold on any longer. All my strength was gone. The reality of the cross left me lying on the floor sobbing. I wept and wept. Tear after tear mixed with snot poured down my nose, leaving a messy pool on the floor. I stayed there, unable to lift myself off the ground, for what seemed like forever.

Then He came to me. The King. He picked me up and held me like a child. He rocked me as I continued to cry into His shoulder. I was a mess, but He did not seem to mind.

"I love You, I love You, I love You," was all I could mutter through my tears.

Finally, He spoke. "My daughter, come, let's get up off the floor now. You don't have to stay like this."

He helped me stand up. Taking my hands as He pulled me up, suddenly I felt invigorated. I felt a renewed rush of strength. I laughed! I don't know why I laughed, but suddenly I just laughed.

"There! There's your joy! In My presence is fullness of joy!" He said.

Together we laughed at that, because Jesus knew it was my favorite scripture.

Just like that, I was suddenly back on my couch in my living room. My body was drenched with sweat. Any amount of makeup I had managed to put on that morning was now washed away. And all I could do was smile. "Wow, God! Wow! Take me back there again, please," I said out loud.

> Wave after wave of power and love hit me.
> It pulsated through my body, causing me to
> shrink lower and lower to the ground until I
> was on my knees, just reaching up, hanging on
> to His presence through that doorknob.

The Vine

Never have I experienced a room in heaven that left me as shaken up as this one. For a week, it's all I could think about whenever I tried to pray. When my husband came home from work that night, I cried as I relayed to him the story. I still cry when I share this story. I can never look at the cross the same. It gets so watered down in the gospel that is preached today. The heaviness of what our King went through for us is often long forgotten in today's message.

Later that week, I flipped open to John 15:5. *"I am the vine, you are the branches; he who abides in Me and I in him, he bears much fruit, for apart from Me you can do nothing"* (NASB). I now have new understanding of this scripture. I remember hanging on to that brass doorknob, hanging on to the reality of the cross like my life depended on it. And then His very hands, the One I love lifting me off the ground when I couldn't stand up, replenishing me with fullness of life.

Application

"Abide in Me, and I in you" (John 15:4 NASB). Are we after intimacy, really? It seems easy to get caught up in the whirlwind and excitement of the *"I in you"* part. Of course we all want more of God to be flowing in us and through us, but are we after the heart of God first? Signs, power, and wonders are great, but even Pharaoh's sorcerers did that. We worship a King who desires intimacy with us, and that is what sets Him apart from the rest.

The cross. Oh, the glorious cross! God always had it in His mind when He created us. The trinity always had it in mind when creation was formed. In the very moment that God breathed life into man and molded woman into a perfect helper, He knew what would be His incarnate very last breath of life here on earth. He knew the sacrifice. He always knew the cross was the price for us. It was always part of God's plan. And that, that's what our King died and rose again for. Intimacy.

Of course we all want more of God to be flowing in us and through us, but are we after the heart of God first? Signs, power, and wonders are great, but even Pharaoh's sorcerers did that.

Will you abide in Him? *Abide* means stay, remain, dwell in. In our fast-paced society, just staying fully devoted and focused on one thing nearly seems impossible sometimes. Returning a text while visiting with a friend and also planning our grocery list at the same time seems to be the normal speed of this generation. Our focus is always pulled away by other distractions.

But will you slow down for Jesus? Will you dial down everything else that comes as a distraction and give your full devotion to the One who gave it all for you? Apart from Him, we are nothing. Will you come back to the cross and fall in love with Him again?

Prayer

God, forgive me. Lord, forgive me for everything that gets in the way of me spending time with You. God, You deserve my everything. You deserve my full attention. I'm so sorry that I'm too busy some days to stop and make time for You. I need more of You in my life. I need to know the reality of the cross more. God, I need Your love in a much deeper way. A much, much deeper way. I don't know it enough. I may think I do, but I don't. Would You show me more of Your love? I desire intimacy with You, Father. I need to come back to You, Lord, and make You number one in my life. Thank You so much, Jesus. Thank You so much for the cross. What You went through there I will never fully grasp. God, You are worth it all. Thank You that You always had me in mind. I love You, Father. Amen.

Discussion Questions

1. Why do you think God told me I didn't know His love in heaven?

Chapter 12

Tips and Training

So now begins your journey of learning to see in the supernatural. You may have started reading this book having already had a few experiences with seeing into the spiritual realm, or you may have had none at all. Regardless of your previous experience, I hope you are now walking more encouraged and with more confidence that this gift of seeing is for you too.

Here are some tips I give people who often ask me, "How do I start seeing?"

Get a Journal

Even if you don't currently enjoy writing in a journal, go and buy one. It will help to be able to go back and see your own progress by looking through your journals. Often we forget details of events, such as where we were when we saw that or had that encounter or what was the feeling when we walked into that room, etc. I have years of journals that have words circled like *I felt, I heard, I saw, angelic encounter, in heaven today, He said, Holy Spirit showed me, I touched, healing, I smelled, prophetic words, I dreamed,* and *I sensed.* After those words I always write down the details of the experience.

This helps easily track my own journey with seeing in the supernatural and track what Holy Spirit is up to daily. Sometimes God releases promises for events or times in the future, so it's great to have those written down to later refer to.

Recently, I stepped into a new role as the associate director of our Healing Rooms here at our church. During a time when our team was worshiping before we were going to minister, I had an angelic encounter. With my eyes closed during worship, I saw a *huge angel* come up to me carrying what looked like a large rubber stamp. He stamped my head, and I felt the weighty presence of the Lord come over me—so much that I couldn't move. As he stamped my head, he told me, "I've stamped you with the mark of *authority* and *leadership.*"

Following that, I heard the Lord's voice say, "Let no man stop what I have set in place." Then the angel was gone. It took me a while to even be able to move from my seat. Immediately, I picked up my journal and frantically scribbled everything down from that encounter.

This was the week that we were relaunching the Healing Rooms and ministry and changing a few ways the Healing Rooms operated. Have you ever heard the expression, "If you step out in the Kingdom, be prepared for a battle?" Well, that week I felt like I was in a battlefield. Complaints about the new changes being made rained down on me and began to suck away my joy and faith that these changes were truly what God wanted for the ministry.

As I went to the Lord about it in prayer, He reminded me to look back over my journal. Believe it or not, I had totally forgotten about this encounter during the week. Reading over it not only encouraged me to keep pressing forward with the changes as God had directed me, but also helped me to remain grounded when more complaints came.

Meet with Jesus, the Father, and Holy Spirit

It's comical that I even have to write this here, but I find that in our fast-paced society we often need the reminder to carve out time in our schedule to meet with the Lord.

Daily, set aside a time to meet God. Take one of the characters of the Trinity, such as Holy Spirit, and ask Him to meet with you today. (Get your journal ready, of course.) Then the next day, ask the Father to meet with you, etc. It's funny, but often even my experiences with seeing can be different based on what character of the Trinity meets with me. Yes, they are three in One, but it is often interesting how we can relate differently to each one based on our own personal walk in life.

So carve out a time when you are meeting the Lord solely through asking for God to encounter you and experiencing Him through your senses. I'm not advising to stop reading your

Bible or worshiping Jesus or however else you encounter God. What I am advising here, is to *be intentional with your time* as you start training in the gift of seeing. Take even ten minutes a day where you solely encounter one of the characters of the Trinity through using your senses alone.

Receive Impartation

When I was first starting out in the gift of seeing, I did not have anyone to help instruct me. No one I knew in the church was walking in seer anointing and could explain to me the encounters I was having. My mother is a seer but only sees the angelic light and heavenly experiences, and she could not really help me understand the demonic stuff I was seeing on people or when doing ministry. Also, the words of knowledge I would get for people or see on people's foreheads as I was praying for them were pretty unheard of in the church at the time. So I trudged through learning about seer anointing on my own for many years. Any book that I could get my hands on that had explanation of seer anointing I read over and over, hoping to ingest understanding. As I trained more in the gift of seeing, the Lord would graciously send me people who were prophetic and also could see in the Spirit to pray over me and encourage me.

This is why I encourage anyone who is a seer or starting to walk in the gift *to get prayed for and imparted to by like-spirited people!* Seers can often feel alone, which the enemy uses to isolate and discourage them from using this powerful gift. So read everything you can about the seer anointing and the prophetic, and then search for a mentor or find mentors at conferences who can pray and impart to you.

Remove Distractions

If you're like me, it's hard to get my mind to just settle sometimes. I am a busy mom of two, and I find myself juggling many things just on a daily basis. When I finally do get a moment to myself, I am still often making lists in my head of things I'm needing to get done once the kids get up from their naps, etc.

So, try this as a simple practice. Close your eyes, let out a deep breath, and ask Holy Spirit to come help you quiet your mind. When I first started trying this, I often would find myself still thinking of other things I could be doing. So I carried a pad of paper next to me so that I could jot down whatever random thought floated through my mind and then jump back into quieting my mind to meet with Jesus.

Hearing God's voice is often the battle of learning to just quiet our minds. It's not necessary to get into a quiet, meditative state to start seeing in the supernatural. Often, it does help people when they are first starting out, though.

Release Creativity

For this next tip, I have no clear explanation of why it helps and is a tool to seeing in the supernatural. Do something that is a creative expression of art. Whether that be dance, draw, paint, play with sand, etc. Ask Holy Spirit to come into this time between you and the Lord, put on some worship music, and create.

Once you've done that for a while, stop and quiet your mind and ask the Lord to open your seer's eyes and show you something in the Spirit. For whatever reason, I have found that releasing creativity often helps people who otherwise felt a block when trying to see.

Seer Training

Imagine you are beginning to lift weights for the first time. At first the repetitions of lifting weights might seem pointless. After time, though, as your muscles grow stronger and you are able to increase the weight you are lifting, those repetitions don't seem as pointless.

It's the same with training in the gift of seeing. Not all of us start out having full-on visions of angels and heaven from the Lord, but rather what I like to call "glances." It's like the Lord allows us to get just a small glance at His presence. In Exodus 33, the Lord passes by Moses in the cleft of a rock and shows him a small ounce of His glory. These types of encounters are often what we experience when we first start out training with the gift of seeing.

When I first started seeing angels at the age of five, they were as real and present to me as any other person standing right next to me talking. But then the gift of seeing just all together stopped for me until I was in my twenties. Some days I saw full angels walking around, but most of the time I would see small impressions from the Lord. I would notice a glow or light behind someone and know that the Lord's presence was resting on them at the time. I would see just a quick impression of the shadow of a lion walking through the room, and then quickly it would be gone. Occasionally I would see a dark cloud over someone's head or around them if they were sick. Often I would also see color changes in a room—like suddenly I would see a beam of bright blue move throughout the room, and then it would be gone. I give these examples not to say this is exactly what it will be like for you when you start training in seer anointing. It's meant rather to encourage you, in case you have had similar experiences and thought you were alone in this, that you are on the right track. You are beginning to see in the Spirit.

Not all of us start out having full-on visions of angels and heaven from the Lord, but rather what I like to call "glances."

Take time weekly to practice seeing in the Spirit. If you attend church, during worship is a great time to practice. Holy Spirit's presence and angels usually come during our heartfelt praise, so this is a perfect training ground. Look around the room and ask yourself, *What do I see right now?* Ask Holy Spirit to open your spiritual eyes and then just wait.

Another concept to keep in mind is that you might not see with your literal eyes but see through another one of your senses. I mentioned a little bit about this in the first chapter already. Humans have six senses—seeing, smelling, hearing, tasting, touching, and sensing being the sixth. So often when we think of seeing in the Spirit, we primarily associate the gift with using our eyes only. I want to challenge your notion of that. Sometimes I see things in the spirit using a sense other than my actual eyes—such as my nose. I usually smell witchcraft before I see it. (It has a distinct smell to me.) Or, when praying for someone, my hand begins to feel hot to the touch when I know the Lord's presence is moving there, healing. These are just other ways the Lord allows me to "see" Him. I have also had the experience where I'll suddenly taste a sweetness that comes so randomly that I know it has to Jesus' presence.

So when you are training in the gift of seeing, don't forget to practice using all your senses. If I go to heaven with God, often I will ask Him to take me back next time to the same place and allow me to see more. As an example, God used to take me to a certain place in heaven that looked like an open grass field and had a large oak tree that I would sit under and meet with Jesus. The first couple of times God took me there, all I could do was see the grass. As I asked Him to open my spiritual eyes more, though, I began to feel the literal blades and dampness of the grass beneath my feet. Then I began to also smell the fresh, wet grass. Finally, I was able to feel the temperature of the air. Sensing all of this didn't happen over-night for me. *It was as I asked God for more ability to see with all my senses that He opened that up for me.*

At an early age, I recognized that my firstborn child is a seer. As I mentioned in a previous chapter, I was busy nursing her one day when an angel walked into the room. She pulled off nursing from me, looked right at the angel, and the two of them began to giggle together. It was the most beautiful, mys-terious moment for me as a new mom. Other times, if we are out in public with her and she sees someone who is carrying something demonic on them, she immediately looks at them and shies away from them, even to the point of throwing a fit if they try to come up and touch her or talk to her. Once when we had an outpouring of His presence fall in our living room, my daughter was actually the first one to see it. She kept walking into our hallway by our living room and looking up. She did it so much, I finally stopped what I was doing and went over to investigate what it was she was seeing. Immediately, I saw an open hole leading up to heaven on the top of the ceiling.

Often we forget just how sensitive children can be. So I try to play "I spy" with her from a seer's perspective. We'll sit or lay on a blanket, ask Holy Spirit to come, and then I ask her to point and tell me what she sees. Sometimes she'll pretend she sees a hippo or elephant in the sky, but other times she'll look in the exact same area I see an angel, point at it, and smile. Just as I make it a goal of mine to practice "seeing" with my daughter, so should we in the same simple, childlike manner.

Creativity Prayer

One thing I have discovered the more I have taught on seer anointing is that there is often a common link between people who cannot see in the spirit but want to and their creativity being blocked. Sounds confusing, right? Well, let me explain. Creative expression and the ability to see in the spirit often go hand and hand. Perhaps the link is the use of the right side of our brain.

Often, our natural creative abilities get squashed down early on in our childhood or sometimes also later on in life. Perhaps as a boy you enjoyed drawing or dancing but were discouraged from pursuing these passions. Perhaps as a young girl you found yourself loving painting or singing but were encouraged to be more like your other sibling who was heady or book smart. Often, the discouragement of creative gifts, or even encouragement or pushing in the direction of more left-brained ways of thinking or being, shuts down our own ability to see in the spirit without our realization.

I was teaching on this very subject one time, and a man who was in his mid-40s had one of those "ah-hah!" moments. It's like I could see a light bulb go on or a switch being turned on for him. He explained to me that as a young boy he was categorized by other peers and his own parents as being "brainy." In a way, he took this on as his identity and pursued his books and studying very seriously. He later worked for years in an environment and job that was very left-brained, linear thinking. So we prayed together for the creative side of his brain to be renewed, called to life, and restored to him. He shared with me then that when he was a child he actually remembered liking to sketch. I encouraged him to pick up sketching again and then ask Holy Spirit to meet him there in those moments and open his eyes. *Through tapping into his creative side again, the Lord opened his eyes to see in the spiritual realm.*

As you read this, if you feel like what I am writing here resonates with you and that perhaps there was once a time in your life when your creative mind or gifting was squashed or not encouraged, I have the following prayer for you to read:

Holy Spirit, I ask You right now to come. Lord, You are a creative God, and You like creativity. I remember a time and believe my own creativity ceased or lessened at this point. So right now, God, I ask You to restore and renew my creative mind. Lord, give me the ability to create again using the right side of my brain.

Right now, pause and ask the Lord to show you a picture or give you insight into one thing you can do that is creative to begin again with.

> *Thank You, Father. I am going to start doing, and no matter the result or what I do or make I thank You because I know You are in it. I release myself from a performance spirit right now, and even if I do art and make a mess it will be glorious because it is for You! Even if I try dancing or singing and it turns out funny looking or slightly hideous sounding, I thank You, Lord, because You love it and are in it.*

I encourage everyone who is pursing the gift of seeing to incorporate a time for a creative outlet as well. Drawing often helps me to turn off the worries of the day. If I am having one of those days when I am finding it hard to really lock in with the Lord and hear clearly or see clearly, I'll spend ten minutes drawing whatever comes to mind and then ask the Lord to open my eyes and speak to me.

Chapter 13

Frequent Questions When Starting

What If I Don't Understand What I Am Seeing?

I will be the first to admit that quite often I don't know what it is I am seeing. Sometimes, the Lord will speak to me by showing me something and then later giving me the revelation on it. I always write down what I see. There have been many times when I will come across a book and an author is speaking directly about something I have seen in the past and gives explanation on it that I would otherwise not have. (Rick Joyner is one who comes to mind as an example of this.) Or I'll be at a church and a guest prophetic speaker will come and give a word that is a total explanation of something I saw previously.

Also, occasionally I have had a vision that is for a regional area and not just for a specific person. I love road trips, and often as I'm driving with my husband and we enter into a new city I will see what feels like a random picture to me, but actually makes sense once I learn the city's history. Once when I lived in Brazil as a missionary, I went sightseeing with friends. As we walked around the city of Ouro Preto, I saw this random impression of what looked like a large cement block and a person standing on top of it. Later on, I discovered that where I saw that vision was an old slavery trading block. As the Lord allows us to see what is over a regional area, it reveals to us strongholds that may still exist, how to pray for an area, and insight into how to minister there.

Once when I was in Nepal, the Lord gave me a vision as our team was praying before we left for ministry time. I saw what looked like an open square. There was demonic presence in every corner of the square. One large demon looked right at me and had the word *depression* written across his chest. There was also a small girl I saw hiding in a corner, but when I looked at the child her face actually looked back at me as an old woman. I had absolutely no idea what this vision was about when I had it at the time. So I just asked God for revelation, wrote it down, and went on to minister with my team.

That day, we went to Durbar square to minister, which was a large temple area. Idolatry and spiritual witchcraft was a strong presence there. Through a crazy alignment of things that only the Lord could do, we actually got invited into a sacred temple to pray for an uncle of a princess. Turns out once we went through his little store front, we were inside that exact square I had seen in my vision the previous day. As I looked up at a window up above, I saw the young girl, who was a mere child, looking down at me. This girl was a princess whom people worshiped as a god. Taken and raised in the palace at a young age, she was never allowed to be outside of the temple, never allowed to be without spot, never allowed to really be a child. That day, I was so thankful that the Lord had allowed me to see that vision ahead of time, because then I really knew how to minister and how to intercede when our team was in there.

Finally, do not feel afraid of what you see if you don't have clear understanding of it. Not everything is a demon, and we should be more concerned with what the Lord is up to than focused on what the devil is up to. It gets dangerous when new seers step into the habit of wondering if everything they are seeing is a demonic presence. They become inundated with fear and center their attention on the devil instead of where it should be, which is on God.

How Do I Know If This Is From God or My Own Soul?

Often, I get asked this question. How can we know for sure if what we are seeing isn't just a random fabrication of our imagination and this is really from the Lord?

My answer isn't the most straightforward one. I would pose this question back, "How can you know for sure if you are hearing the Lord's voice?" You can't. It's something learned. There are times that I know that I know that I heard Lord's voice clearly, and other times just take faith. The more you develop your gifting, the more you will be able to discern what is from the Lord and what is not, just as you learn to hear His voice with accuracy.

Since the whole new age movement took off, people are understandably a bit shy about using their imagination for the Kingdom. The enemy wrapped his talons around something that is supposed to be beautiful, something that the Lord put in us to use. Think about it—if God created man and woman, do you think He wouldn't want us to use our own creativity and imagination to get in touch with Him? Let's take fear out of the picture when coming to meet with the King and let go and let God! I've seen, more often than not, that our actual fear of not truly seeing clearly from the Lord stifles people from even trying.

Pray before you start that the enemy would not enter into this time between you and the Lord. Also, let go of any fear you might have to just make mistakes. It's a learning curve, and you can give yourself grace in the process.

Always test what you are seeing with Scripture to make sure it lines up with the nature of Christ. It's not uncommon for the enemy at first to try and step into your times of seeing with the Lord. If you are questioning it, ask yourself, *How does this make me feel right now?* If you are feeling something that is outside of the nature of Christ—such as fear, pain, discomfort, even confusion sometimes—it's probably not the Lord and possibly your own flesh.

Then some pose the question, "But what if I see something demonic?" It's true. You might see something demonic on a person or even a demon walking around the room during a ministry time. If you do see a demon, it's not your chance to point at a person and critically tell them, "I see you are carrying such and such a spirit!" The Lord reveals demonic presence to us in His loving kindness. We gain direction in ministering by seeing them and also ability to see the spiritual warfare that might be present. It's always been my experience that the Lord shows me demonic presence to bring about freedom. Let's not be quick to judge someone else because you might see a demonic something on them. Let's get real. Our battle is not of flesh and blood but against principalities. As long as we are here on earth, we've all at some point probably had a demonic something on us. We all need to be cleansed in the blood and need the grace and forgiveness of God in our lives.

So don't be afraid when or if you see something demonic. The Lord's the one allowing you to see it for a specific reason. Place your focus on Him, and ask Him what He wants you to do with that vision. And always remember, that demon is secretly intimidated by *you* because you are made in the image of Christ and you carry the very power and authority of the cross!

I always tell people—check back with Scripture and make sure what you are hearing or seeing lines up with the very nature of Christ. Would Christ want to show you this? Why is Christ allowing you to see this?

I See This. Now What?

Hopefully by now, after reading this book, the Lord's beginning to open your spiritual eyes more and is talking to you through the gift of seeing. Not all visions are for you to act on. Granted, some images you will see are just a private message between you and the Lord. In ministry though, the Lord might show you a picture or image for someone else. Just as every prophetic word has a season, it is the same with the seer anointing. Not all images or pictures I see are for now. The Lord might be giving me prophetic knowledge about a person, but I always ask Him if the vision is for me to share now, before I share it. Even if the Lord shows me I can share it, I always tread carefully with the person in front of me. Something I might say is, "The Lord was just showing me a picture of this…. I'm not sure if this relates to you but what I think the Lord was showing me about that is…. Do you relate to that at all, or does that resonate anything inside of you?" I find this model or way of talking about a vision tends to take the weirdness out of it and allows the person you are ministering to to feel like your heart is for them, not against them. Also, it helps them feel like they are in control and you are not coming at them with a "Thus sayeth the Lord" type attitude.

By staying afraid, we aren't able to step
out in our gifting, and so we cannot make
war on the enemy of this world.

So as you step out in your seer anointing and begin to experience more, pray and ask the Lord for wisdom with each encounter. Is this something for you to share right now, or is it for later? How should you share it? Could this possibly be just wisdom from the Lord that gives you direction as to how to pray or minister? As you lean into Holy Spirit, He will show you what to do.

What If I'm Afraid?

First, I cast no judgment on you. When I first started seeing in the spirit, I didn't have anyone to help me navigate through the visions I was seeing or what I was sensing. I often felt isolated and alone in it all. Especially when I would see things and have no understanding or way to explain it to friends, I struggled a little with fear.

The more I learn about the Lord and about the seer anointing, the more I learn that the enemy tries to make believers get stuck in our fear. By staying afraid, we aren't able to step out in our gifting, and so we cannot make war on the enemy of this world.

John 14:27 says, *"Peace I leave with you; My peace I give to you; not as the world gives do I give to you. Do not let your heart be troubled, nor let it be fearful."*

Second Timothy 1:7 says, *"For God has not given us a spirit of timidity, but of power and love and discipline."*

So remember, you are covered in the blood of Christ. No weapon formed against you shall prosper. You are not alone in seeing, but the enemy would like you to believe you are. *Fear is not in heaven. I know, I've been there!* So where is this fear coming from right now? If you are experiencing any form of fear or anxiety when seeing something, break the power of fear in Jesus' name. Then ask the Lord to only allow you to see what you are ready for or what He wants you to grow in.

Chapter 14

What to Expect

After reading through this book and doing all the applications and prayers at the end of the chapters, you should gain more sensitivity to Holy Spirit and be able to start seeing into the supernatural with the Lord. Here are a few things you can expect.

Expect to sense what's in the atmosphere as well. The more the Lord started to open my seer anointing, the more often I would walk into an environment and start picking up what was in the room. Sadness or anxiety would come on me as I walked into a coffee shop, whereas previously I had been feeling completely happy. For a while, I didn't realize what was going on, but later it helped me to realize that I was sensing what was in the atmosphere and that it wasn't my own to claim.

Expect to see glimpses and not always full angels or pictures. As I train more and more (and I'm always learning), the Lord sometimes would just show me part of an image or a glimpse, as I mentioned previously. So don't get discouraged if you are not seeing full images or visions yet. Just keep watching and always asking for more.

Matthew 7:7 says, *"Ask, and it will be given to you...knock, and it will be opened."* God wants us to participate with Him! God always surprises me, but that doesn't mean I am to not participate and sit back and just allow God to show up. I want more of the giftings; I want more of Him! So I am always asking for more. As you align yourself with the Lord, pray, worship Him, read your Bible, and set aside time to meet with Him, expect Him to show up. The time you are willing to devote and practice seeing will determine the spiritual muscles you will gain. Expect the Lord to meet your desire and hunger to see.

> The time you are willing to devote and practice seeing will determine the spiritual muscles you will gain. Expect the Lord to meet your desire and hunger to see.

Everyone goes through a dry season with the gift of seeing. I have yet to meet a seer who doesn't admit to this. Our own flesh might get in the way, our own sin, or our own busyness and lack of ability to recognize Him amidst our schedules. But then there are also dry seasons seers go through simply just because. The Lord might be trying to take you in a different direction—like a season of simply rest, or a season to just focus on your family, etc. It doesn't mean that the gift of seeing won't return. With the gift of seeing, I've noticed a pattern in my own life of dry seasons, explosion seasons, and then steady seasons. I just do my part to make sure there is nothing I personally have done to cause the dry season, and I press into Him. But we all go through it. Don't worry. You will go through an explosion season or steady season with seeing again.

People may not understand you. I advise every seer to find Spirit-filled mentors who are prophetic. Also, pray for the Lord to show you who you can share with about seer anointing. If you can find another seer to run alongside you as you learn, do it! It's the best thing you can do to grow in the gift.

I mentioned this previously, but I feel like it's an important point to reiterate. Often, you may have a vision that is not for an individual or for yourself, but rather a corporate vision or picture for a region. So always ask the Lord to give you revelation on what you are seeing before you jump to try and come up with your own understanding.

Expect the Lord to speak to you more through your dream life. Dreaming is a way of seeing too. I always record in my journal all my dreams that I feel are from the Lord, even if I don't understand them at the time. You've asked the Lord to open your eyes, so now expect Him to also begin to start helping you see even through your dream life.

With spiritual growth might come spiritual attack as well. I remember having a vision where the Lord would be confirming a direction for me, and then directly after that or the next day something would happen to make me question if I was seeing or hearing the Lord correctly. Sometimes also the Lord may show you something so that when you are in a rougher season when warfare is intense, you can look back on what He showed you and be encouraged. As you step out and ask for more, don't be surprised if there might be spiritual attack. Claim it all as victory, and keep going after the gift! Know that you are on the right track, put on the full armor of Christ, and keep asking for more.

This should go without saying, but expect *glory!* Expect to encounter the Lord in new ways that reveal more about Him to you, get you more excited to meet with Him, and help you feel closer to the Lord. Every time I get to experience part of heaven, I never get tired of it. I am always asking for more and am more in awe of Jesus every time.

Chapter 15

Room of His Lavishing Love

It's one of my favorite rooms. It's one of those that I just cannot get enough of! Don't get me wrong—all rooms in heaven are amazing. This one, though, holds a special place in my heart. It is one of the first places God ever took me to in heaven. I call this room the room of *lavishing love*. It's where I go most frequently with the Lord when I need to replenish, when I need a touch from Him.

So there I was, back in Brazil doing ministry with the ex-street children from the slums. Often, I would find myself drained—literally drained! Emotionally, spiritually, and physically I would feel at my end. (Now, I know that putting ministry before everything else is not God's way, but I was a lot younger then and more naïve.) So I asked the Lord one day to take me somewhere new. I asked him to open my eyes to see Him more because I desperately needed to see Him.

Then it happened. I was suddenly not in my room anymore but in a different room. At first, it scared me because I didn't know what had just happened. But then I saw Him. Jesus was standing in the middle of the room smiling at me, shin deep in water. He motioned for me to come walk out toward Him, so I trudged through the water to where He was standing. He smiled and then was gone. Just like that!

"You can't turn that faucet off! That's My overflowing love pouring out of there, and it can't be turned off."

There I was in this new and exciting place in heaven. Water was everywhere! That was the first thing I noticed when I came to this room. Water came up to my shins, and at some points when I walked around it came up to my knees. The water was constantly moving, but there never seemed to be a source for the current. It moved, but I could stand my ground without toppling over. This water was unlike any other current I have ever seen here on earth. It was warm to touch—just the right temperature, actually. The color of the water was like a swirling rainbow. Hues of blue, turquoise, green, gold, and at times purple all swirled around. Water also climbed the walls and dripped from the entire ceiling like honey. As it dripped down on my head and back, I didn't feel wet, but as each drop touched my body I felt a zing of energy and warmth. Truly, it was unlike anything I have ever seen or experienced before.

The room felt warm in temperature. Not too hot and yet not too cold. Just perfect, actually! When I breathed in, I smelled something super sweet. Almost like pomegranates, honey, and flowers mixed together. The smell was unlike any other scent I had ever smelled before. I could feel Holy Spirit buzzing about the room. It is hard to describe. Although there was just me in the room, I could sense someone else's presence, and the room felt busy. The constant movement of the water, colors, and air made the room feel alive with excitement.

On the right side of the room, I could see something that sat up about three and a half feet out of the water. As I trudged through the waters to get closer to it, I could see that it came up to my chest level. There sat a porcelain sink. It wasn't beautiful by any means, but was just a traditional square looking wash sink. I saw that the spigot had been left on, so I went to try and turn it off. I turned as hard as I could. "Agh!" I sighed out loud. The spigot could not be turned off. Water was overfilling the sink and overflowing onto the ground. So, I tried again. No success! I tried a third time, and that's when I heard His voice.

"Ana, you can't turn that faucet off! That's My overflowing love pouring out of there, and it can't be turned off. You are stepping in it, breathing it in, and covered in it. You won't ever be able to turn My love off!"

Whoa! I was undone by that. That is when I realized how amazing I felt in that room. Ever since I got there I had felt so energized, so full of life, joy, happiness, and peace that I hadn't felt before. So, I decided to go for a swim! *Why not?* I thought. *Let's soak up all the love of God I can while I'm here!*

Just like that, I forgot the reason I had asked God to take me to heaven in the first place.

So, I swam, I splashed, I skipped, I even washed my hair in it, and it felt amazing. I was having the time of my life when suddenly something else caught my eye in the room. There in the far left corner I saw something I hadn't seen before. I saw a giant mirror.

I went as fast as I could—running, which is nearly impossible in shin-deep water. The mirror was a long, oval mirror with gold trim. I sat before it in the water and dared to peer in. At first all I saw was my own reflection. I thought, *What is this Lord? You are showing me this in heaven when it's something I could see any day on earth?* Thankfully, God is patient with me.

Then I heard, "Look deeper."

So I kept looking, and that's when I saw the image start changing. Like a watercolor painting at first, my face started transforming, and then suddenly I saw Jesus smiling back at me. Those eyes! There's nothing in the whole world like those eyes. Nothing more beautiful, more joyous, and more alive than those eyes.

I smiled back at Him with tears in my own eyes. The very sight of Him smiling at me left my heart melted. The worries of that day were gone in that second. Just like that, I forgot the reason I had asked God to take me to heaven in the first place. All I wanted to do was sit before that mirror forever and look into those eyes smiling at me. It was breathtaking. Words fail me right now to describe how it felt. It lasted only a few seconds but seemed like eternity.

Then, the image started to change again. Hues of red and orange and fiery amber came through, and then suddenly I was looking at the Lion of Judah. At first I felt afraid, but then when I looked into His eyes I could see the Father coming through them, and so I felt loved and safe. The Lion smiled at me and then roared! The strength of that roar shook my entire being. The busyness of the room seemed to stop in that moment. I felt stress completely leave my body in that moment. It's hard to describe, but it felt almost like I came into that room of heaven carrying a heavy load on my back, and after the Lion of Judah roared something broke off of me in the spiritual realm. I felt light and free and so happy.

And then, just like that, I was back in my room in Brazil.

You are privileged that the Lord has chosen you to do that, but it's never really about you.

Conclusion

There is nothing like His presence. The greatness of Him, His love, and the power of God is enough to stop any ambition we have. A room in heaven stopped for the King; how much more should we!

From the beginning of time, on the sixth day God looked into man's face He had just formed and smiled and said, "It is good." From the very beginning, God has desired intimacy with us. Was He lonely? *No!* Did He need us? *No.*

Often, we get confused about the order of things. "But God, if I don't build this house for these children, no one will care about them! But God, You are calling me to speak to this church. If I don't go, what will happen to the people there?" Don't get me wrong. God speaks to each one of us and often calls us to do great things for His Kingdom. But when our motive moves us to a place where we are trying to do things for pleasing Him or because we feel like He needs us, we have accidentally bumped into partnering with a spirit that is not Jesus' heart.

His heart from the beginning was intimacy. That's it! Intimacy! "But God, I have to do this!" No, you don't! You are privileged that the Lord has chosen you to do that, but it's never really about you. Let's get our hearts in check.

My husband and I went to India with all the wrong thoughts at first. Our intentions were great, but our hearts were not. OK, so we truly felt like God had called us to go and start up a ministry working in the sex trafficking, red-light area in that city—a great and worthy call. We met with countless ministries there that had been working there for years. We researched a bunch of different areas to begin our ministry. Nothing would open up for us, though! It was frustrating, taxing, and felt hopeless. *What are we doing wrong?* we thought. Our hearts weren't right. We were still operating out of that place of doing things for the King, instead of being with the King. So He shut the doors. It took many hopeless months of trying before we finally got it. And guess what? Jesus actually was calling us to go to Nepal to just be with Him. There we partnered alongside Iris Ministries.

Yes, we did miracles and saw people healed and come to Jesus weekly, but more than that we learned to just be. And you know what? My heart came alive. More alive than it's probably ever felt. I wasn't looking for the ministry to fulfill my heart, which was good because every ministry has it's up and down days, but the King was meeting me daily.

> We do because we feel like it connects us to Him when all He ever wanted was intimacy.

It was always interesting watching the tourists who would come into Calcutta when we lived there. Around the areas that Mother Theresa's homes are set up and still operating, there you can always find lots of tourists. Hundreds of thousands of tourists come through there yearly, seeking to have some heightened spiritual experience or connectivity to the universe. No matter what their religious background, whether they are looking for God or not, in some way they are looking! People everywhere are looking, looking for purpose—an answer to the questions, *Do I really matter? What was I created for? Does anyone truly know me and see me?* Disconnectedness with the Father breeds an empty and purposeless feeling. Sadly, many people operate still out of this place in ministry. Doing instead of being with the King becomes a norm. We do because we feel like it connects us to Him when all He ever wanted was intimacy. A crisis hits and suddenly identity issues get stirred up for us. Nothing we do can make Him love us any less or more. That reality always hits me afresh every time the Father takes me back to the room in heaven of lavishing love.

It is the same with the gift of seeing in the spirit or anything supernatural. If our motive for seeing in the spirit is for self-promotion or to gain an amazing story, then our hearts are in the wrong place. Our motives are impure. All He ever wants is to connect with us. All the King requires is our heart—our whole heart. Not fragments of it, nor our perfect heart. All He wants is our weak little heart to be completely surrendered to Him. And then He comes. He interrupts our little lives, our little imperfect lives, just to build relationship with us. For this, and for this alone, we pursue the gift of seeing.

When was the last time you sat with the King? When was the last time you sat with Jesus and asked Him what He thought of you? When was the last time you sat completely still with Holy Spirit and asked Him to show you new things? Our society is constantly pressing for things *now!* The repercussion of this in the body is a generation of lovers who can't just sit still with the Lord—a generation that can't just empty themselves completely to be filled up completely by Him.

> He interrupts our little lives, our little imperfect
> lives, just to build relationship with us. For this,
> and for this alone, we pursue the gift of seeing.

The more I see in the supernatural with God, the more I desire. I have gone through dry seasons of not seeing also. These seasons are usually because I am not connecting enough with Him. I am distracted from my one true purpose. It is out of our love for Him that we must seek to see Him. It's out of our desire to draw near the King that we should run after the supernatural. *"As the deer pants...so my soul pants for You"* (Ps. 42:1). It's out of our desire to know Him and make Him known that we must press into the gift of seeing.

Three simple questions are worthy to ponder on. When is the last time you truly sat with Him and listened? Are you really desperate? What's standing in the way of you accomplishing these first two questions?

Prayer Application

God, make us hungry for You. God, mark me as one who is desperate to know You more. The more I learn You, the more I want to know more about You. I want nothing else to stand in the way of getting to know You. I am thirsty for You, Lord.

Forgive me, Lord, for any time I pursued my own selfish motives above Yours. How great are Your ways, God. Your ways are so much better than mine ever could be. God, I want to surrender my will to You right now. I want to empty myself completely so that You can fill me up. I want to be so full of You that I can't help splashing onto others with Your love. God, I desire intimacy with You.

Lord, I want to see You more. Open my eyes right now to see into the spirit. Come invade my times with You. Please come and interrupt my life over and over again! I want to see more of You, God. I want to see what's on Your heart for today. Would You trust me with that? Right now, I place my own hands over my own eyes and call them forth to see in the supernatural with God. Eyes, in the name of Jesus, I say open! God, I'm here, laying my heart bare before You, asking You to move in it in a new way. Move in my life, God. Draw closer to me so that I may draw closer to You. I love You, Lord. Amen.

Discussion Questions

1. Do you ever find yourself caught up in operating out of a performance spirit—doing instead of being?

2. In what way do you need to slow down and just *be*?

About Ana Werner

Ana Werner and her husband Sam, are the Associate Directors of the Heartland Healing Rooms in Lees Summit, Missouri, and also founders of Acacia Ministries International. Ana travels and equips people internationally on seeing in the Spirit, moving in the prophetic, and healing ministry. Her transparency as she shares on the realities and experiences she has in heaven, bring Holy Spirit, the love of the Father and the power of God into the room when she speaks. Ana is passionate about leading people into encountering Jesus' heart. To learn more about Ana's ministry, please visit anawerner.org.